Early Childhood Environment Rating Scale

THIRD EDITION

Thelma Harms   **Richard M. Clifford**   **Debby Cryer**

Teachers College, Columbia University
New York and London

Published by Teachers College Press, 1234 Amsterdam Avenue, New York, NY 10027

Cover design by Turner McCollum

ISBN 978-0-8077-5570-9

Printed on acid-free paper
Manufactured in the United States of America

22 21 20 19 18 17 16 15   8 7 6 5 4 3 2 1

Contents

Acknowledgments

We are grateful to the many colleagues who have contributed to this Third Edition of the ECERS. From the very beginning of our work on the scales, we sought input from practitioners in the field, as well as from experts in child development and in the provision of learning environments for young children. We have received literally thousands of thought-provoking comments and questions about the ERS family of instruments on our website (www.ersi.info). In addition, we have worked with many colleagues in research and training efforts. Each of these experiences has molded our views of how early childhood environments affect young children's development across the full range of developmental needs. Although it is impossible to mention each one who contributed ideas during the many years that the ECERS has been in use, we want to express our gratitude first to each of the many people who have given us feedback, both informally and formally. This includes colleagues in the United States as well as around the world whose work in research and program improvement with the ECERS has added greatly to our understanding of quality.

We want to recognize in particular:

- Our colleagues at the Environment Rating Scales Institute who have generously shared their insights resulting from many years of training and collecting data. Specifically, thanks are due to Cathy Riley, Tracy Link, Lakeisha Neal, Lisa Waller, and the many consultants who work with them.

- Researchers at Frank Porter Graham Child Development Institute, University of North Carolina at Chapel Hill who gathered large data sets and conducted research on the ECERS-R that helped guide our detailed review of each Indicator and Item during the revision process. Special thanks go to John Sideris, Jen Neitzel, and Stephanie Reszka for leading this work.

- Researchers from both Frank Porter Graham Child Development Institute and other research organizations who so generously shared data with us as we prepared for this revision, including Donna Bryant, Noreen Yazejian, Ellen Peisner-Feinberg, all from FPG; Steve Barnett and Ellen Frede from the National Institute for Early Education Research at Rutgers; and Deborah Cassidy and Linda Hestenes from the University of North Carolina at Greensboro.

- Our colleagues at the Branagh Information Group for their help and crucial support during the field tests with preparation of Tablet PC software to allow for data collection in their system, as well as ongoing support as we developed the analysis data set for use in our field tests. Mark Branagh and Mary Frances Lynch deserve special thanks.

- Bud Harrelson and Dari Jigjidsuren for serving so capably as study coordinator and data analyst for the ECERS-3 field test. Without their help the study would not have been possible.

- The agencies and individuals who volunteered their time and effort to collect ECERS-3 reliability data during the two field tests: Georgia Department of Early Care and Learning (Melissa Davis, Denise Jenson, Nakilia McCray, and Margaret Stephens), Tulane University (Angela Keyes and Faith Boudreaux), Pennsylvania Keys to Quality (Jill Kortright, Angela Mamrack, and Bobbi Philson), the ERSI folks listed above, and individuals (Rogers Hewitt, Janine Joseph, Gail Lindsey, and Judy Scott).

- Professor Kathy Sylva (Oxford University) and the members of the International ECERS Network for their inspiration and insights into the use of the ERS instruments in widely differing international settings and the implications for revisions in this Third Edition of ECERS.

- Colleagues and translators with whom we have worked closely to make the ECERS available in various languages. Their work has inspired us to regularly examine the critical elements of learning environments as these concepts play out in various cultural and ethnic settings.

- Our colleagues at Teachers College Press, including the editors and staff as we have worked together toward this new edition. Their support and encouragement has helped keep us moving forward..

- The many teachers and administrators who have welcomed us into their programs and classrooms, particularly those who helped with the pilot and field tests in 2013 and 2014.

—Thelma Harms, Richard M. Clifford, and Debby Cryer, August, 2014

Introduction to the ECERS-3

The Third Edition of the ECERS is a major revision that introduces innovations in both the content and administration of the scale while retaining the continuity of the two principal characteristics of the ECERS, namely its comprehensive or global definition of *quality* and the reliance on *observation* as the primary source of information on which to base assessment of classroom quality. We continue to maintain a comprehensive view of early childhood development that includes physical, social-emotional, and cognitive domains, as well as children's health and safety. We see the physical environment, children's relationships with one another and with significant adults, and instruction as intertwined. Much of teaching is done during the course of the day as teachers interact with children at play and during routines.

The original ECERS (Harms & Clifford, 1980) contained 37 Items organized in 7 Subscales. Each Item was presented as a 7-point Likert Scale with four quality levels, each level defined by a descriptive paragraph. The ECERS-Revised Edition (Harms, Clifford, & Cryer, 1998,) consisted of 43 Items organized in 7 subscales. In the Revised Edition, each level of each Item was defined by numbered Indicators, thus making it possible to more clearly assign scores and to use the assessment to more precisely guide program improvement. The ECERS-R Updated version (Harms, Clifford, & Cryer, 2005) contained the same 43 Items and Subscales, but with greatly expanded notes for clarification and an expanded Scoresheet. It is this updated ECERS-R version that we used as the basis for the completely revised Third Edition. We have maintained the use of Indicators evaluated on the basis of classroom observation, but have significantly revised the Indicators and the Items they comprise in order to reflect current knowledge and practice in the field.

In terms of scoring the ECERS-3, we have maintained the basic approach of scoring the set of Yes/No Indicators of quality and basing the 1–7-point Item scores on the Indicator scores. In addition, we have maintained six of the seven subscales from ECERS-R, eliminating the Parents and Staff subscale because of limited variation in scores and the complete dependence of scoring on teacher reports rather than observation. A total score is also calculated in the same manner as in ECERS-R. Further, we now recommend that all Indicators be scored regardless of the Item score in order to provide a more complete view of quality. In the near future we will provide online access to a new scoring system similar to the newly released scoring program for ECERS-R.

This combination of continuity and innovation has enabled the ECERS to serve as the most widely used early childhood environment quality assessment instrument in the United States and worldwide—used in more than 20 countries and formally published in 16 of those countries, with additional translations currently underway.

Our revision process included consideration of current literature on child development, early childhood curriculum, and emergent classroom challenges, such as appropriate use of technology, as well as health, safety, and facility recommendations. While the wide list of resource material used in this process is too lengthy for inclusion in this Introduction, several deserve special mention. With a greater emphasis on cognitive development, including both language, mathematics, and science, the following were all pivotal in guiding our revisions: National Association for the Educations of Young Children's [NAEYC] revision of *Developmentally Appropriate Practice* (Copple & Bredekamp, 2009) and *Developmentally Appropriate Practice: Focus on Preschoolers* (Copple et al., 2013); the National Council of Teachers of Mathematics position statement, *What Is Important in Early Childhood Mathematics?* (2007; n.d.); *Mathematics Learning in Early Childhood* (National Research Council, 2009); the joint position statement on technology and interactive media tools of NAEYC and the Fred Rogers Center for Early Learning and Children's Media at Saint Vincent College (2012); *Preventing Reading Difficulties in Young Children* (National Research Council, 1998); ASTM International's Standard Consumer Safety Performance Specification for Playground Equipment for Public Use (2014); *Caring for Our Children: National Health and Safety Performance Standards* (American Academy of Pediatrics, American Public Health Association, & National Resource Center for Health and Safety in Child Care and Early Education, 2011); and the U.S. Consumer Product Safety Commission's *Public Playground Safety Handbook* (2008).

A second major source of information that guided our revision process was a study of a large sample of classrooms assessed with the ECERS-R. Working with colleagues at Frank Porter Graham Child Development Institute, we were able to examine in detail the functioning of the ECERS-R Indicators and Items. Gordon and colleagues (2013) noted that there was some disordering in the placement of Indicators along the 1–7 continuum of quality and that some Indicators were actually measuring more than one domain of quality, but were only counted in one domain, resulting in loss of information. In the large data set we accumulated, we were able to identify the specific Indicators of concern and eventually arrive at an alternate set of subscales and a new scoring system for ECERS-R. Based on this work, we adjusted the location of key indicators in ECERS-3, modified the Indicators themselves, and added new Indicators to improve the scaling. We are also recommending that all Indicators in ECERS-3 be scored, even when this is not necessary to determine a given Item's score.

A final and critical source of information for revision of the scale was the close contact and open communication we have maintained with practitioners in the field, including classroom teaching staff, program directors, licensing agencies, technical assistance providers, college and other training faculty, and in particular with our close colleagues at ERSI, who provide training and reliability determination to users of the ERS materials across the United States. (See the Acknowledgements section for more details on the extensive support we have received from the field.) The experience of the authors in observing programs first-hand, training observers, conducting research, and working with local, state, and national officials on Quality Rating and Improvement Systems all have had an impact on this edition as well.

What is substantially different in the ECERS-3rd Edition (2015) from the ECERS-R Updated (2005) Edition?

- ECERS-R considers what is observed during the observation as well as teacher reports about the rest of the day to determine scores for a number of Items.
- ECERS-3 considers only what is observed during a 3-hour time sample to determine scores for all Items dealing with the ongoing program, such as the activities, interactions, and language. Additional time may be added only to review materials or the safety features of the playground.
- ECERS-R has 43 Items organized in 7 Subscales: Space and Furnishings, Personal Care Routines, Language-Reasoning, Activities, Interaction, Program Structure, and Parents and Staff.
- ECERS-3 has 35 Items organized in 6 Subscales: Space and Furnishings, Personal Care Routines, Language and Literacy, Learning Activities, Interactions, and Program Structure. The Parents and Staff Subscale has been dropped because it relies mainly on teacher or staff reports, not on observations. Several other items that are often not observed, such as Greeting/departing and Nap/rest, have been dropped or modified.
- ECERS-R requires close attention to examine the number and quality of accessible materials.
- ECERS-3 requires less attention to accessible materials and more attention to how the teachers use the materials to stimulate children's learning.
- ECERS-R contains 4 Items on "Language-Reasoning"
- ECERS-3 contains 5 new Items on "Language and Literacy," with more specific Indicators provided in order to assess teacher strategies for guiding language and literacy awareness.
- ECERS-R contains 10 Items to assess "Activities" of different types
- ECERS-3 contains 3 new Math Items (23, 24, and 25) that focus on helping children become familiar with math. Item 23, Math materials and activities, considers the materials children play with and learn from, and the math-related activities offered in the classroom with the intent of pointing out math concepts. Item 24, Math in daily events, focuses on making children aware that math is part of our daily lives, is present even when we are not playing with math materials, and is used under meaningful daily life circumstances. Item 25, Understanding written numbers, focuses on becoming familiar with the math symbols and understanding what they mean.

Final minor modifications were made based on the field test results. We eliminated 7 Indicators with low reliability and revised the Notes for Clarification for several other Indicators in order to improve their reliability.

Reliability and Validity of the ECERS-3

As noted earlier in this document, the ECERS-3 is a revision of the widely used and documented *Early Childhood Environment Rating Scale* (ECERS), one in a family of instruments designed to assess the overall quality of early childhood programs. Together, these scales have been used in major research projects in the United States, as well as in a number of other countries. With only few exceptions (e.g., Sabol & Pianta, 2014), extensive research has documented both the ability of the scales to be used reliably and the validity of the scales in terms of their relation to other measures of quality and their ties to child development outcomes for children in classrooms with varying environmental ratings (Aboud & Hossain, 2011; Burchinal, Kainz & Cai, 2011; Burchinal, Peisner-Feinberg, Pianta, & Howes, 2002; Cryer et al., 1999; Gordon et al., 2013; Harms, Clifford, & Cryer, 2005; Helburn, 1995; Henry et al., 2004; Pinto, Pessanha, & Aguiar, 2013; Love et al., 2004; Sabol & Pianta, 2013; Sylva et al., 2004; Whitebook, Howes, & Phillips, 1989). Some of the studies show the effect of high quality as measured by the ERS instruments persists well into elementary school (Peisner-Feinberg et al., 1999), or secondary school (Sammons et al., 2011). However the relationship between overall global quality and specific child outcomes for ECERS-R, as well as other measures of child care quality, is relatively small (Burchinal et al., 2011). This new edition, ECERS-3, is designed to improve prediction of child outcomes while maintaining the emphasis on the importance of a wide range of developmental outcomes in children.

Since the concurrent and predictive validity of the ECERS-R is well established, and the current revision maintains the basic properties of the original instrument, the focus of the first field studies of the ECERS-3 has been on the degree to which the Third Edition maintains the ability of trained observers to use the scale reliably. Additional studies will be needed to document the continued relationship with other measures of quality, as well as to document its ability to predict child outcomes. As further studies are completed, these will be posted on the ERSI website (www.ersi.info).

After extensive revision, the authors conducted small pilot trials of the ECERS-3 in the summer of 2013, and a larger field test of the scale that autumn. The results of this field test indicated that further refinements in the ECERS-3 were needed. Subsequently, the authors completed another round of revisions in the first half of 2014 and launched a second field test in the late spring. In this second field test, a group of volunteer observers who were proficient in use of the earlier ECERS-R received training in the new ECERS-3, including field practice in which they demonstrated adequate levels of reliability. All 14 assessors attained reliability of 85% agreement within one point on the 35 Items of the scale. Thirteen of these observers were able to attain this level of reliability with a gold standard trainer in their first two joint observations in real-life classrooms operating normally. The 14th assessor took two additional trials to get to reliability. After attaining this baseline reliability, the trained assessors were paired with one another in order to conduct the reliability study. It should be noted that these assessors were all very experienced in using the ERS instruments. One should expect a more extensive training period will be needed to train assessors new to these instruments.

The sample of classrooms in the study consisted of 50 classrooms in 4 states— Georgia (12), Louisiana (4), North Carolina (24), and Pennsylvania (10). Classrooms were recruited with a goal of having approximately 1/3 of the total be low-quality programs, 1/3 be of mid-level quality, and 1/3 be of high quality, based on available data from state licensing and Quality Rating and Improvement System information. In the end, the sample is somewhat skewed, with relatively few high-scoring classrooms and more in the moderate- to low-scoring range, but adequate distribution was attained to allow for examination of use of the scale across the wide range of quality of programs available in these states. Results of the study are presented below. Assessors were rotated to the extent possible to ensure that reliability was measured across multiple assessor pairs. In each classroom two assessors rated the classroom environment independently of one another, but at the same time. The core assessment took place during a prime time of the day for exactly 3 hours, with some additional time allowed to examine the gross motor area if it was not used during the observation, and to examine materials in the classroom that were not able to be assessed during the formal observation period. In both of these added times, ratings were only allowed for the very specific Items in Gross Motor Space and Equipment, and in the Indicators related to the materials. All measures of child and teacher interactions were based on the 3-hour segment.

Indicator Reliability. Indicator reliability is the proportion or percentage of scores that exactly match for each Indicator by the two assessors independently completing ECERS-3. Across the 35 Items in the ECERS-3, there are a total of 468 Indicators. The Indicators were scored either *Yes* or *No*, with several Indicators allowed to be assigned a *NA* (not applicable) in certain circumstances. Assessors were instructed to score all Indicators for each classroom. The average reliability across all of the Indicators and assessor pairs was 88.71%. A few Indicators scored below 75%. Subsequent to the field test, the authors examined those Indicators to either eliminate the Indicators or to make minor adjustments that would improve the reliability.

Item Reliability. Because of the nature of the scoring system, it is theoretically possible to have high Indicator agreement but low agreement at the Item level. Two measures of Item agreement have been calculated. First we calculated the agreement between pairs of observers within 1 point on the 7-point scale. For the full 35 Items, exact agreement occurred in 67% of the cases, and agreement within 1 point was obtained in 91% of the cases. Item agreement within 1 point ranged from a low of 82% for Item 3, Room arrangement for play and learning, to 98% for Item 25, Understanding written numbers. Subscale scores within 1 point ranged from 88% for Program Structure to 100% for Learning Activities.

A second more conservative measure of reliability is Cohen's Kappa. This measure takes into account the difference between scores. The mean Kappa for the 35 Items was .54. Kappa's ranged from a low of .18 for Item 3, Room arrangement for play and learning, to a high of .84 for Item 27, Use of technology. Only 2 Items had Kappa's below .40 (Item 3, Room arrangement for play and learning, and Item 6, Space for gross motor play, with a kappa of .35). In both cases, the mean Item score was extremely low. A characteristic of the Kappa statistic is that for Items with little variability, the reliability is particularly sensitive to even minor differences between observers. The authors and observers agreed that the low scores on these Items accurately reflected the situation in the groups observed, and that any changes to substantially increase variability would provide an inaccurate picture of the features of quality reflected in these two Items. The edits made for Indicators discussed above should result in a somewhat higher kappa for the low-scoring Items without changing its basic content. These changes are included in the published version of the scale. Even using this more conservative measure of reliability, the overall results indicate an acceptable level of reliability for the instrument as a whole.

Intraclass Correlation. A third way of looking at reliability, intraclass correlation, looks at the level of agreement between observers when they assess quality independently. It accounts for both the correlation between two observers and also takes into account differences in the absolute magnitude of the two assessors' ratings. We assessed the absolute agreement intraclass correlation coefficient in a two-way mixed model, average estimates, where 0 represents no correlation between assessments and 1 represents perfect correlation. At the Item level the mean coefficient was .90, with a range from .664 for Item 3, Room arrangement for play and learning, to .965 for Item 30, Staff–child interaction. Coefficients for the subscales are shown in the table below. Generally correlations of .85 or higher are considered acceptable. As can be seen in the following table, average item, subscale, and total scale scores exceed this expectation.

Intraclass Correlations of Subscales

Subscale	Correlation
Space and Furnishings	.93
Personal Care Routines	.94
Language and Literacy	.96
Learning Activities	.97
Interaction	.98
Program Structure	.96
Full Scale (Items 1–35)	**.90**

Internal Consistency. Finally we examined the scale for internal consistency. This is a measure of the degree to which the full scale and the subscales appear to be measuring common concepts. Overall, the scale has a high level of internal consistency, with a Cronbach's alpha of .93. This figure indicates a high degree of confidence that a unified concept which we call *quality of the environment* is being measured. A second issue is the degree to which the subscales also show consistency—that is, are they measuring some construct consistently? Below is a table showing the Cronbach's alphas for each subscale:

Internal Consistency

Subscale	Cronbach's Alpha
Space and Furnishings	.93
Personal Care Routines	.91
Language and Literacy	.91
Learning Activities	.93
Interaction	.96
Program Structure	.87
Full Scale (Items 1–35)	**.93**

Cronbach's alphas of .6 and higher are generally considered acceptable levels of internal consistency. Overall the field test demonstrated a high level of inter-rater agreement across the scale items and at the full-scale score level. These findings are quite comparable to those found in similar studies of the ITERS-R and the ECERS-R, except that the subscales seem to be more stable measures of their respective concepts than in previous editions of the ECERS and ITERS. All of these previous studies have been confirmed by the work of other researchers not related to the authors, as described at the beginning of this section, and the scales have proven to be quite useful in a wide range of studies involving the quality of environments for young children. At the same time the scales have been shown to be user-friendly to the extent that it is possible to get observers to acceptable levels of reliability with a reasonable level of training and supervision. While the Cohen's kappa measure of reliability was lower than would be preferred, in total, this set of analyses clearly supports the ability of the scale to be used reliably in real-world settings.

We have not presented normative data here because of the small sample size and the restricted geographic coverage. Such data will be posted on the ERSI website (www.ersi.info) as it becomes available.

While the authors are fully responsible for the content of this section, we recognize the major contributions of Bud Harrelson, who served as the study coordinator, and of Dr. Dari Jigjidsuren, who conducted the statistical analyses.

References

Aboud, F. E., & Hossain, K. (2011). The impact of preprimary school on primary school achievement in Bangladesh. *Early Childhood Research Quarterly, 26*, 237–246. doi: 10.1016/j.ecresq.2010.07.001

American Academy of Pediatrics, American Public Health Association, & National Resource Center for Health and Safety in Child Care and Early Education. (2011). *Caring for our children: National health and safety performance standards; Guidelines for early care and education programs (3rd ed.).* Elk Grove Village, IL: American Academy of Pediatrics; Washington, DC: American Public Health Association.

ASTM International. (2014). *ASTM 1487-11 standard consumer safety performance specification for playground equipment for public use.* Available at www.astm.org/DATA-BASE.CART/STD_REFERENCE/F1487.htm

Burchinal, M., Kainz, K., & Cai, Y. (2011). How well do our measures of quality predict child outcomes? A meta-analysis of data from large-scale studies of early childhood settings. In M. Zaslow, I. Martinez-Beck, K. Tout, & T. Halle (Eds.), *Quality measurement in early childhood settings* (pp. 11–32). Baltimore, MD: Brookes Publishing Company.

Burchinal, M. R., Peisner-Feinberg, E., Pianta, R., & Howes, C. (2002). Development of academic skills from preschool through second grade: Family and classroom predictors of developmental trajectories. *Journal of School Psychology, 40*(5), 415–436. doi: 10.1016/S0022-4405(02)00107-3.

Copple, C., & Bredekamp, S. (Eds.). (2009). *Developmentally appropriate practice in early childhood programs serving children from birth through age 8* (3rd ed.). Washington, DC: National Association for the Education of Young Children.

Copple, C., Bredekamp, S., Koralek, D., & Charner, K. (Eds.). (2013). *Developmentally Appropriate Practice: Focus on preschoolers*. Washington, DC: National Association for the Education of Young Children.

Cryer, D., Tietze, W., Burchinal, M., Leal, T., & Palacios, J. (1999). Predicting process quality from structural quality in preschool programs: A cross-country comparison. *Early Childhood Research Quarterly, 14*(3).

Gordon, R. A., Fujimoto, K., Kaestner, R., Korenman, S., & Abner, K. (2013). An assessment of the validity of the ECERS-R with implications for assessments of child care quality and its relation to child development. *Developmental Psychology, 49*(1), 146–160. doi: 10.1037/a0027899

Harms, T., & Clifford, R. M. (1980). *Early Childhood Environment Rating Scale*. New York, NY: Teachers College Press.

Harms, T., Clifford, R., & Cryer, D. (1998). *Early Childhood Environment Rating Scale, Revised Edition*. New York, NY: Teachers College Press.

Harms, T., Clifford, R., & Cryer, D. (2005). *Early Childhood Environment Rating Scale, Revised Edition, Updated*. New York, NY: Teachers College Press.

Helburn, S. (Ed.). (1995). Cost, quality and child outcomes in child care centers: Technical report. Denver, CO: University of Colorado, Department of Economics, Center for Research in Economic Social Policy.

Henry, G., Ponder, B., Rickman, D., Mashburn, A., Henderson, L., & Gordon, C. (2004, December). *An evaluation of the implementation of Georgia's pre-k program: Report of the findings from the Georgia early childhood study (2002–03)*. Atlanta, GA: Georgia State University, School of Policy Studies, Applied Research Center.

Love, J. M., Constantine, J., Paulsell, D., Boller, K., Ross, C., Raikes, H., . . . & Brooks-Gunn, J. (2004). *The role of Early Head Start programs in addressing the child care needs of low-income families with infants and toddlers: Influences on child care use and quality*. Washington, DC: U.S. Department of Health and Human Services.

National Association for the Education of Young Children. (2009). *Developmentally appropriate practice in early childhood programs serving children from birth through age 8: A position statement of the National Association for the Education of Young Children*. Washington, DC: Author. Available at www.naeyc.org/positionstatements/dap

National Association for the Education of Young Children, & the Fred Rogers Center for Early Learning and Children's Media at Saint Vincent College. (2012). Technology and interactive media as tools in early childhood programs serving children from birth through age 8. Available at www.naeyc.org/files/naeyc/PS_technology_WEB.pdf

National Council of Teachers of Mathematics. (2007). What is important in early childhood mathematics? Available at www.nctm.org/standards/content.aspx?id=7564

National Council of Teachers of Mathematics. (n.d.). Executive summary: Principles and standards for school mathematics. Available at www.nctm.org/uploadedFiles/Math_Standards/12752_exec_pssm.pdf

National Research Council. (1998). *Preventing reading difficulties in young children*. Washington, DC: The National Academies Press.

National Research Council. (2009). *Mathematics learning in early childhood: Paths toward excellence and equity* Committee on Early Childhood Mathematics, C. T. Cross, T. A. Woods, & H. Schweingruber (Eds.). Center for Education, Division of Behavioral and Social Sciences and Education. Washington, DC: The National Academies Press.

Peisner-Feinberg, E. S., Burchinal, M. R., Clifford, R. M., Culkin, M. L., Howes, C., Kagan, S. L., Yazejian, N., Byler, P., Rustici, J., & Zelazo, J. (1999). The children of the cost, quality and child outcomes in child care centers study go to school: Technical report. Chapel Hill, NC: University of North Carolina at Chapel Hill, Frank Porter Graham Child Development Center.

Pinto, A. I., Pessanha, M., & Aguair, C. (2013). Effects of home environment and center-based child care quality on children's language, communication and literacy outcomes. *Early Childhood Research Quarterly, 28*, 94–101.

Sabol, T. J., & Pianta, R. C. (2013). Can rating pre-K programs predict children's learning? *Science, 341*(6148), 845–846.

Sabol, T. J., & Pianta, R. C. (2014). Do standard measures of preschool quality used in statewide policy predict school readiness? *Education Finance and Policy, 9*(2), 116–164.

Sammons, P., Sylva, K., Melhuish, E., Siraj-Blatchford, I., Taggart, B., Draghici, D., Toth, K., & Smees, R. (2011). *Effective Pre-School, Primary and Secondary Education Project (EPPSE 3-14) influences on students' development in key stage 3: Social-behavioural outcomes in year 9 full report*. London, England: EPPSE Project, Institute of Education.

Sylva, K., Melhuish, E., Sammons, P., Siraj-Blatchford, I., & Taggart, B. (2004). *The Effective Provision of Pre-School Education (EPPE) project: Final report: A longitudinal study funded by the DfES 1997–2004*. London, England: Institute of Education, University of London/Department for Education and Skills/Sure Start.

U.S. Consumer Product Safety Commission. (2008). *Public Playground Safety Handbook*. Available at www.cpsc.gov/PageFiles/122149/325.pdf

Whitebook, M., Howes, C., & Phillips, D. (1989). *Who cares? Child care teachers and the quality of care in America*. National child care staffing study. Oakland, CA: Child Care Employee Project.

Notes

Administration of the Scale

1. This scale is designed for use with one classroom or one group at a time, for children aged 3 through 5 years of age. If at least 75% of the children in the group are at least 3 years of age, use this scale. For younger groups, use the ITERS. Unless stated in the Indicator, all Indicators apply to all children. However, it is not necessary to ensure that each and every child receives the required experiences from the environment provided. One must observe what happens and determine whether the experiences are likely to occur for all the children in the group.

2. **A block of at least 3 hours should be set aside for the observation, with additional time added as needed to more closely examine materials and gross motor area(s).** The observation should take place during the time when most children are likely to be present and not during arrival and departure times unless the program is 3 or fewer hours in duration. If a game operates for 3 or fewer hours, observe during the whole time.

The 3 hours are a "time sample" in which all that is observed during that period will determine the score for all Items and Indicators. For example, if there is no free play during the 3-hour time sample, mark any indicators requiring free play as a negative score (either a *Yes* for the Inadequate level of quality (1) or a *No* at higher levels of quality (3–7). Similarly, if no gross motor play is observed during the 3-hour time sample, do not give credit for any Indicators related to gross motor. The following classroom observation procedures should be adhered to:

- The observation should take place during the most active part of the day, when most children would be expected to be in attendance.
- If you arrive before most children are in their regular classroom with their regular teaching staff, delay the 3-hour time sample until the regular group begins and at least half of the children are present. You may use the time to examine materials or gross motor space(s).
- It is permitted to stay for a longer period, for example, to observe and score specific routines that did not occur during the time sample, or to look more closely at materials/equipment that children could access during the 3-hour observation, but were not seen due to a lack of time. In addition, gross motor space and stationary equipment should be observed if these were not evident during the observation. However, when scoring routines or checking on materials, observed evidence (such as interactions and activities) that occurs after the time sample is over should not be counted towards meeting scale requirements.

- **A staff interview is not used** when scoring this scale. All scores are based on observation. However, before beginning the observation, ask questions of program staff to gather the information on the first page of the score sheet. You will need this preliminary information for scoring and to identify program characteristics.
- Follow the group being observed, wherever they go. If a class is separated into two or more groups to go to different areas, follow just one group, and base scores on what those children experience. For example, if one half of the children go outside to play and the other half remain inside for indoor activities, follow one group only. Remember that the two groups will probably have different experiences, but the score will be based on the group you followed.
- A typical observation generally takes place in the morning, between 8:30 and 11:30 or 9:00 and 12:00. However, it is helpful to contact the program before visiting to obtain information that will help determine the best time to complete the observation. For part-day programs, the observation should take place during the time when most children are likely to be present and not during arrival and departure times, unless the program is less than 3 hours. If a program operates for less than 3 hours, observe during the whole time, and reduce the time required for "accessibility" to 20 minutes.
- Do not observe special supplementary classes that are not offered to the whole group. For example, do not follow children whose families have made special arrangements for dance, gymnastics, or computer that are not part of the regular program.

3. When you arrive at the program, and before beginning the observation, complete as much of the identifying information at the top of the first page of the Scoresheet as possible. You will have to ask the program staff for information. Make sure all identifying information is completed.

4. An **Observed Schedule** is required to calculate amounts of time during which children are engaged in the varying activities provided in the classroom, such as:

- when and for how long specific materials are accessible for use by the children,
- length of waiting times, if any,
- length of group times,

Begin the **Observed Schedule** immediately upon arrival into the classroom.

Continue to note times as the 3 hours progress, noting what children are experiencing for each period recorded. For example, if you entered a classroom at 8:36, and the children were waiting for circle to begin, having snack, or engaged in free play with all or a portion of materials, you would write this on the Observed Schedule, noting what children were able to access. Remember that some materials might be accessible for more time than others.

In order to calculate whether required amounts of time were provided for children, it is best to wear a digital watch. Even though required times are a minimum, because of possible timing error, we allow a 2-minute exception because it is so difficult to track time to the second. However, no more than 2 minutes can be found to be lacking to meet time requirements.

Finalize scores requiring examples of interactions, such as talking done by staff or other staff behaviors, during the observation only after the 3 hours have ended unless you have already found the examples needed to assign a score. Score other aspects of interactions not requiring specific examples based on the total 3-hour observation time, and determine a score close to the end of the time sample.

5. You will need to move around the space(s) used by the children during the observation. This is to ensure accurate scoring for materials and interactions. Make sure you can hear what teachers and children say in conversations or other talking observed. Pay special attention to collecting information that can only be observed at a limited time, such as requirements in Meals/snack, Toileting/diapering, or circle time.

Follow these **Observer Guidelines** for appropriate behavior during an observation:

Affect the environment as little as possible

• Teachers/providers will be involved with the children during your observation and should not be asked to talk with you or answer questions. You should obtain the required program identification information before entering the classroom, or from the teacher upon entering the room. However, if the teacher is engaged and should not be interrupted, wait until there is a reasonable time to get the information needed.

• As an observer you may acknowledge children if they approach you. If they ask, you can tell them that you are watching them play today, or that you have to finish your work. Do not otherwise take part in their activities or interact with them.

• Do not interfere with ongoing activities in any way. Station yourself around the perimeter of the rooms, as unobtrusively as possible, but move periodically to collect evidence needed for accurate scoring.

• If it does not interfere with the ongoing program, you may sit in a chair or on the floor. Do not sit on other furniture, such as shelves, tables, the children's chairs near an activity table, or on play equipment.

• Move if you are in the way of adults or children. Remain sensitive to what is happening around you.

• You may look at materials that are in plain view on open shelves, if you can do so without disturbing the group. Do not look through drawers, in cabinets, or in other closed spaces that are not accessed and used by the children.

• Do not leave tote bags or purses within reach of children. It is best not to take them into the classroom.

• Have your cell phone turned off unless an emergency situation exists.

• If working with another observer in the room, refrain from talking during the observation.

• Try to keep a neutral facial expression so that children and/or staff are neither drawn to you nor concerned about your response to them.

• Handwashing or use of a hand sanitizer is required for all ERS observers upon entering the program.

6. Definitive, nationally recognized resources are used when scoring health and safety items in the scale. There are specific handouts that give the requirements needed in order to score accurately. Have with you, preferably attached in the scale, the following resources:

• In order to use current information in assessing gross motor space and equipment, use the **Playground Information to Use with the Environment Rating Scales**. The content of this handout is based on information from the *Consumer Product Safety Commission (CPSC) Public Playground Safety Handbook*, Pub. No 325 and the American Society for Testing and Materials Standards (ASTM). The handout is available on the Environment Rating Scales Institute (ERSI) website, www.ersi.info. It is listed under the "Supplementary Materials" tab for each scale.

• The nutritional content of the Meals/snacks item depends on the USDA food pattern guidelines. Use the handout, **USDA Meal Guidelines Ages 1-12**, available on the ERSI website.

• Health information from the publication *Caring for Our Children* is available in the additional Notes for Clarification of Items and in the next section.

entitled "Explanation of Terms Used Throughout the Scale." *Caring for Our Children* is available online at www.cfoc.nrckids.org.

- Interpretation of the requirements in the scales is updated in the Additional Notes for Clarification. The notes are available at www.ersi.info. This website should be checked regularly and the new notes should be printed out and attached to relevant pages in the scale.

7. Use time efficiently when completing the scale. All Indicators and Items should be scored before leaving the facility. Observers should spend most of the time looking for evidence and checking off Indicators as evidence is found, rather than taking voluminous notes and deciding on scores after leaving the facility. During the observation, take notes on the Scoresheet to support your scoring decisions. For example, if staff must be observed making at least one type of comment, note the example observed in order to ensure that assumptions are not being used to generate a score. If an example is not observed, do not give credit.

Scoring System

1. Read the entire scale carefully, including the Items and the Notes for Clarification. In order to be accurate, all ratings have to be based as exactly as possible on the Indicators provided in the scale Items.
2. The scale should be kept readily available and consulted frequently during the entire observation in order to make sure that the scores are assigned accurately.
3. Examples that differ from those given in the Indicators but that seem comparable may be used as a basis for giving credit for an Indicator.
4. Scores should be based on the current situation that is observed.
5. When scoring an Item, always start reading from 1 (inadequate) and progress upward, scoring each Indicator *Yes* or *No*.
6. Ratings are to be assigned in the following way:
    - A rating of 1 must be given if any Indicator under 1 is scored *Yes*.
    - A rating of 2 is given when all Indicators under 1 are scored *No* and at least half of the Indicators under 3 are scored *Yes*.
    - A rating of 3 is given when all Indicators under 1 are scored *No* and all Indicators under 3 are scored *Yes*.
    - A rating of 4 is given when all Indicators under 3 are met and at least half of the Indicators under 5 are scored *Yes*.
    - A rating of 5 is given when all Indicators under 5 are scored *Yes*.
    - A rating of 6 is given when all Indicators under 5 are met and at least half of the Indicators under 7 are scored *Yes*.

- A rating of 7 is given when all Indicators under 7 are scored *Yes*.

A score of *NA* (Not Applicable) may only be given for Indicators or for entire Items when "NA permitted" is shown on the scale and on the Scoresheet. Indicators that are scored *NA* are not counted when determining the rating for an Item, and Items scored *NA* are not counted when calculating subscale and total scale scores.

7. To calculate average subscale scores, sum the scores for each Item in the subscale and divide by the number of Items scored. The total mean score is the sum of all Item scores for the entire scale divided by the number of Items scored.

While it is sometimes possible to determine an Item score without completing all of the Indicator scores for the Item, the authors highly recommend scoring all Indicators for all Items when using the scale. This practice provides a wealth of information for program improvement and technical assistance to programs. Further, having this complete information facilitates data analysis and research activities. It also reduces problems with missing data. Recently, an alternative scoring method for ECERS-R has been developed that requires all Indicators to be scored. It is anticipated that a similar alternative scoring option for ECERS-3 will be available in the near future.

Use of the Scoresheet and the Profile

The Scoresheet provides for both Indicator and Item scores. The Indicator scores are Y (Yes), N (No), and NA (Not Applicable), which is permitted only as noted for selected Indicators. The Item scores are 1 (Inadequate) through 7 (Excellent), and NA (Not Applicable), which is permitted only as noted for selected Items. Care should be taken to mark the correct box under Y, N, or NA for each Indicator. The numerical Item score should be circled clearly.

The Scoresheet included in this edition can be used as both a worksheet and a Scoresheet. In addition to the spaces provided for notes, there are questions, charts, and other aids for keeping track of specific information gathered throughout the observation. For example, the number of child-sized chairs and tables, the number of times handwashing is completed, or examples of various categories of materials can be conveniently recorded and calculated directly on the Scoresheet.

The Profile on page 13 of the Scoresheet permits a graphic representation of the scores for all Items and subscales. It can be used to compare areas of strength and weakness, and to select Items and subscales to target for improvement. There is also space for the mean subscale scores. The profiles for at least two observations can be plotted side by side to present changes visually.

Explanation of Terms Used Throughout the Scale

1. **Accessible** means that children can reach and use the materials, furnishings, equipment, and so forth, in question. There should be no barriers to children's access. Barriers to access can be physical, such as when furniture blocks an area so it is difficult to get to the materials, or if materials are stored in containers with difficult-to-open lids. Staff control can also be a barrier to access, such as by telling children that a center is "closed," teaching children not to take certain materials from shelves, or assigning children to areas so that they cannot move freely to choose something else to play with. Time counted as materials being accessible must be when all children have reasonable access and are not compelled to be doing something else, such as finishing a meal or being in a required group time, or napping while others get to use materials.

- Unless specified in an Item, accessibility must be observed during the observation in order to give credit.
- To determine whether materials are accessible for the amount of time required at the varied quality levels, a time sample of 3 hours should be used. No additional time should be considered to meet the accessibility requirement.
- If children leave the play area to go to a special activity while the rest of the class continues to play, such as a therapy session or to use the toilet, continue to count the time that the materials are accessible. The same is true if children leave to attend classes not provided to all children as part of the regular program, such as computer or gymnastics that parents pay for separately.
- Unless specified in an Item, all materials required in an Indicator must be accessible during the time required.
- The observation must take place when most of the children are likely to be accessible during the most active part of the program day, usually in mid-morning for a full-day program.

For materials to be considered accessible does not mean that every child must have access during all of the time required, but that each child who wishes should have a reasonable chance to use the materials. For example, access may be limited to a certain number of children in an area or limited to certain times of the day. For materials to be considered accessible, they must be within view of younger preschoolers (3's). For older preschoolers (4's and 5's), if materials are stored in closed spaces, they can be considered accessible only if it is *observed* that children can freely access

and use the materials. Generally, for materials to be counted as accessible to children at the Minimal (3) level, children must be able to reach and use the materials for a period of at least 25 minutes during the 3-hour observation. Twenty-five minutes of access is also required when the term "accessible" is used with no stated time requirement at the higher levels of quality. This time can be provided at one time during the observation, or as a combination of several periods. At higher levels of quality (5 and 7), accessibility is required for a period of 1 hour in the 3-hour observation.

Pro-rate the times to give credit for accessibility in programs of less than 3 hours. Use the chart below.

Time Sample Requirement Substitution for Programs of Less Than 3 Hours

	1-hour program	1½-hour program	2-hour program	2½-hour program	3-hour program
For 1-hour requirement:	20 minutes	30 minutes	40 minutes	50 minutes	60 minutes
For 25-minute requirement:	10 minutes	15 minutes	15 minutes	20 minutes	25 minutes

Vigorous gross motor activity is required for children's health. In programs that provide non-gross motor materials (fine motor, art, books, etc.) outdoors, or during indoor gross motor times, credit can be given for access to these non-gross motor materials only if there is time for accessing them in addition to the minimum time needed for vigorous physical activity.

2. **Engaged** means children are interested and paying attention. This should be differentiated from just being well-behaved, but not necessarily engaged. Children may sit quietly and even face the teacher, but unless they show interest in some way, you may not say they are actually engaged. Children may lose their engagement (for example, play with their shoe; chat with a neighbor) but become re-engaged quickly, and this should not carry much power when scoring. It is the longer-term lack of engagement, often associated with a negative staff response, that is most important to consider when scoring.

3. **Hand hygiene.** *Handwashing and hand sanitizer use:* The 2011 edition of *Caring for Our Children* states that hand sanitizers can be used by adults and children 2 years of age and older in place of handwashing unless hands are visibly soiled (p. 113). Therefore, the use of hand sanitizers is acceptable when scoring these Indicators as long as the product contains 60–95% alcohol, manufacturer's instructions are followed, and very close supervision of children is provided to ensure proper use and avoidance of

ingestion or contact with eyes and mucous membranes. Check to be sure that the manufacturer's directions for use are followed exactly. If not, do not give credit. Ask to see the original container with directions for use if it is not observable. If children are not closely supervised when using the sanitizer, consider this in rating supervision-related Indicators for the Item specifically, and also in Safety and Supervision Items.

If hands are visibly dirty, handwashing, according to the required procedure, is still required—although the time for rubbing soapy hands together before rinsing has increased from 10 to 20 seconds. Antibacterial soaps should not be used.

Children using some shared art or sensory materials must wash hands, or use hand sanitizer according to directions, both before and after use. Moist or wet materials are more likely to spread germs than dry materials. For example, shared crayons would not require hand hygiene before or after use, but two children sharing play dough or fingerpainting on one surface would require it. Similarly, hand hygiene would not be required before using shared dry sand (but would be required afterwards), but if water is shared, then hand hygiene is required both before and after use.

4. Individualized teaching involves responding to variation in the abilities, needs, and interests of children in the group; working with individual children in a systematic way that involves determining the child's ability to do a task or learn a concept; providing support and encouragement; using appropriate strategies that respond to the child's needs and interests; and assessing the success of the child in completing the learning task. Ideally this is most often done in an informal manner, with little use of directive teaching strategies. So care must be taken to look for subtle ways that staff interact with children throughout the observation. Clearly, all children should not be expected to do the same thing at the same time as the primary method used.

An observer should expect to see more difficult skills encouraged in older or more advanced children. Even with smaller groups of children, attention must be given to differing ability levels. The observer should look for the success of each child to determine if the teaching is truly responsive and appropriate for each child. Even when there are general expectations for all children, such as children writing their name when they enter the room, the observer must determine the degree to which each child can successfully complete the task to determine if instruction is individualized.

Generally during free play, when children can choose which materials to use, and use them as they are able, individualizing is present in the curriculum. However, individualizing must be observed in the interactions of teachers with the children as they play, as well as in the range of materials that children are taught to use. Staff might encourage a 4- or 5-year-old to use smaller fine motor materials, do more complex tasks, or spend more time on issues of math and literacy in their play. Younger preschoolers should have easier conversations with teachers about their play, and should be appropriately challenged.

5. A **play area** is a space where play materials are provided for children to use. An **interest center** is a clearly defined play area for a particular kind of play. Materials are organized by type and stored so that they are accessible to the children. Furniture is provided for use of the materials, if needed. An appropriate amount of space is provided for the type of play being encouraged by the materials and the number of children allowed to play in the center. Since blocks and dramatic play materials are associated with more active play, interest centers for these materials should likely be larger than for other materials, such as books, science, or fine motor. If the definition of "interest center" is not met, then credit can be given for the space being a "play area" only. "Interest centers" are more specific, clearly distinguished types of play areas. If one or two materials are present that do not match the intent of the center's particular type of play, give credit for an interest center as long as those materials do not interfere with the intent of the interest center. For example, if their use would not take up needed space or adversely affect the noise level required by the center's type of play.

6. Sanitizing and Disinfecting. In order to clarify the different but related functions of cleaning, sanitizing, and disinfecting to remove germs, *Caring for Our Children* states that "cleaning" means physically removing dirt and contamination using soap and water and applying friction, thus exposing any remaining germs on the dry, clean surface. "Sanitizing" means reducing germs on an inanimate surface or object to a safe level. "Disinfecting" means destroying all germs on an inanimate surface or object. A sanitizer should be used on food contact surfaces or any object that is mouthed. A disinfectant should be used only on diaper changing tables, toilets, counter tops, and door and cabinet handles. Only EPA-approved products are acceptable, and all sanitizers and disinfectants must be used according to the instructions on the container. The instructions on the original container of bleach or other commercial product should be followed when preparing sanitizing and disinfecting solutions. In general, bleach/water solutions used as a sanitizer or disinfectant must remain on the surface for at least 2 minutes in order to be given credit, unless it is observed on the original container that a different amount of time is required.

7. Staff generally refers to the adults who are directly involved with the children—the teaching staff. In the scale, staff is used in the plural because there is usually more than one staff member working with a group. When individual staff members handle things differently, it is necessary to arrive at a score that characterizes the overall impact on the children by all the staff members. For example, in a room where one staff member is very verbal and the other is relatively nonverbal, the score is determined by how well the children's needs for verbal input are being met by all staff combined.

In all Items involving any type of interaction, "staff" refers to those adults who are in the classroom and who work with the children daily (or almost daily), for a large part of the day. This can include volunteers, if they are in the classroom for the required amount of time. Adults who are in the classroom for short periods of the day, or who are not a regular daily part of the classroom, do not count in evaluating whether the requirements of the Item are met. For example, if a therapist, parent, or the director of a program comes into the classroom and interacts with children, for short or irregular periods, these interactions do not count in scoring the Item, *unless the interaction is very negative*. As an exception, in parent cooperatives or lab schools, whose usual staffing pattern includes different people as teaching assistants daily, these assistants should be counted as staff.

8. Teaching is an educational interaction between teaching staff and each child, where the teacher provides information and enhances a child's learning and thinking. It can be formal or informal, planned or spontaneous. If staff do not interact with the children, they are not teaching them, although children may well be learning through other avenues—from one another, through exploration and experimentation, and through other experiences.

Teaching can occur at group times, while children play, and during routines or transitions. As long as children are awake, there is a possibility for teaching.

9. Usually and **generally** are terms used to represent the general practice observed, meaning about 75% of the time. However, for interactions Indicators the terms refer to the general practice, with very few exceptions.

10. The term **weather permitting** is used in several Items of the scale with regard to when children can participate in outdoor activities. "Weather permitting" means *almost every day*, unless there is active precipitation, public warnings of extremely hot or cold conditions, or public announcements that advise people to remain indoors due to high levels of pollution that might cause health problems. Children should be dressed properly and taken outdoors on most days. This might require that the schedule be changed to allow children outdoor play in the early morning if it will be very hot later in the day. Or it might require that the program ensure that children have boots and a change of clothes for a day when the grass is wet. After bad weather, staff should check the outdoor area, dry off equipment, sweep away water, or block off puddles as needed, before children go out. Programs with protected outdoor areas, such as a deck or patio, are more likely to be able to meet the requirements for allowing outdoor activity daily, weather permitting

Overview of the Subscales and the Items of the ECERS-3

Notes for Clarification

*Consider only the space(s) used by children during the observation in scoring this Item.

1.1, 3.1, 5.1. "Not enough space" means that there is little room to fit all the furnishings required for basic routine care and learning. For example, few open shelves fit in the space, tables must be crowded together. "Enough indoor space" means that the basic furnishings for play and routines fit reasonably well into the room and children and staff can move around with few problems, even if interest centers might be more crowded than desired; tables and chairs are easily used, but there is little if any extra space to give an open feeling to the room. "Ample indoor space" easily fits all furnishings needed for routines and play, including cubbies and extra furnishings for play, such as a sand table or a woodwork bench. There is a spacious feeling to the room, and only very minor crowding of interest areas or the area used for circle time.

3.3. Do not be overly perfectionistic in scoring this Indicator. Do not consider extremely minor problems, such as slightly frayed carpets, chipped tiles on floors, or small sections with peeling paint where display has been moved.

3.5. Score Yes if all children and adults currently using the indoor space can currently access it. If there are no people with disabilities requiring special access, score Yes.

5.1. To determine whether the space is ample, look for areas where furnishings or children are crowded. For example, watch to see whether the group meeting space allows comfortable space for each child. Make sure interest centers are not crowded, and that there is space for children to access materials without having children sitting in chairs causing difficulties. Check pathways to be sure they are wide enough to work well as children move from place to place. Consider space in the classroom used for nap, only if nap is observed, with 36 inches required as space between cots/mats. If children are somewhat crowded, but generally still comfortable for very short periods (e.g., short circle time), score Yes if there are no other issues that would affect the score.

5.3. When opening windows/doors is the only method of ventilation control used, the windows/doors must have screens, bars, or another appropriate safety feature if they present a danger of children climbing out and falling a significant distance. Score No if such a precaution is not present and there is no other method of moving fresh air into the indoor space.

7.1. Most natural light should be controllable. However, a small window or a door does not require control of natural lighting as long as its light does not create a problem, such as making the room too hot or bright for the activities taking place.

7.2. In order to be accessible for children and adults with disabilities, doorways to the center, classroom, children's bathroom, and playground must meet certain physical requirements. The width of the doorways must be at least 32 inches, the door handles must be easily operated with limited use of hands (such as a lever handle or push bar), and the threshold of the doorway can be no more than 1/2 inch high, and if greater than 1/4 inch high, must be beveled in order to allow a wheelchair to roll over it easily. The need to use stairs is considered here. In addition, entryways used to access the facility must be handicapped accessible—for example, having an easy-to-reach push plate to open the door, or a push plate doorbell in addition to keypads that limit access to the building.

SPACE AND FURNISHINGS

1. Indoor space*

1.1 Not enough space to provide adequate care for the highest number allowed to attend at one time (Ex: basic furniture crowds space so children and staff cannot move freely; crowding causes conflicts among children).*

1.2 Space lacks sufficient lighting, ventilation, temperature control, or is very noisy (Ex: staff or children complain about temperature; staff must talk loudly to be heard above constant noise).

1.3 Space is generally in poor repair (Ex: much peeling paint on walls or chipping plaster; damaged floors; large water stains on ceiling).

1.4 Space is poorly maintained (Ex: floors left sticky or dirty; much built up soil around baseboards or furniture).

3.1 Enough indoor space for children, staff, and basic furnishings for routines, play, and learning.*

3.2 Adequate lighting, ventilation control, comfortable temperature, and reasonable noise level (Ex: staff and children usually talk without raising voices to be heard; room is not stuffy or gloomy).

3.3 Space is generally in good repair (Ex: no major hazards that could cause injury or illness, and few minor problems such as a slightly torn rug or missing sections of the baseboards).*

3.4 Space is reasonably clean and well-maintained.

3.5 Space is accessible to all children and adults currently using the classroom.*

5.1 Ample indoor space that allows children and staff to circulate freely, enough space for mealtimes, group times, and suitable space for activities in free play.*

5.2 Some direct natural lighting through windows or skylights.

5.3 Ventilation can be controlled (Ex: widows can open; fan used by staff).*

7.1 Natural light can be controlled (Ex: adjustable blinds or curtains).*

7.2 Space is accessible to children and adults with disabilities (Ex: ramps and handrails for people needing them; access for wheelchairs and walkers; push-plate doorbell instead of small button).*

7.3 Most indoor surfaces are durable and easy to clean and maintain.

Notes for Clarification

3.1. When considering furnishings for play, there should be enough low open shelves for enough toys to keep children reasonably well-engaged. If materials are inadequate, so not many shelves need to be used, score *No*. The shelves holding the toys and materials should not be crowded.

3.4. Wall-to-wall carpet that covers several areas can count as 2 soft furnishings. For routine care, consider furniture for nap only if nap "set-up" is observed. Assume that the number of cots/mats put out is correct for the number of children who participate in nap.

5.1. Score based on the furnishings required throughout the year. For example, when considering children's storage space, if cubbies are not large enough to hold winter coats, but it is summer and no coats are used, this would not be scored as acceptable if the children's possessions would once touch once coats were added. Similarly, if the program allows 17 children in the classroom at one time, but there are 15 children currently present and only 15 chairs in the room, score *No*.

5.3, 7.2. Do not count multiple pieces of furniture that are designed for the same type of play, such as 2 pieces of housekeeping furniture, 2 sand tables, or 2 separate easels. The furniture must be used during the observation or obviously set up for child use even if no child chooses to use it. Do not count furniture that is considered generic, such as tables and chairs or low open shelves, even if they are used for a specific type of activity. For example, a table with a computer on it is not counted here, but a specially designed computer table would be.

5.4. "A substantial amount of softness" requires that children can mostly escape the typical hardness of early childhood classrooms. Padded or cushioned surfaces must be provided for the children to relax on, with little or no contact with a hard surface. Examples of "a substantial amount of softness" would include several large pillows on a rug, a cushioned couch or chair on a rug (even if the furniture has wooden arms), a small mattress, or a beanbag chair (not deflated) on a rug. Do not count instances where a minimum amount of softness is provided, such as small cushions, a bed pillow on a carpet, or a little upholstered stool.

7.1. To be "convenient," cubbies must be accessible to the children. Teachers/children should not have to leave the room to access cubbies or cots/mats.

Inadequate		Minimal		Good		Excellent
1	2	3	4	5	6	7

2. Furnishings for care, play, and learning

1.1 Not enough basic furniture for routine care, play, and learning (Ex: not enough chairs for all children to use at the same time; very few open shelves for toys; no furniture for storage of children's personal possessions).

1.2 Furniture generally in such poor repair that children could be injured (Ex: splinters or exposed nails; wobbly legs on chairs; cots torn).

1.3 No soft furnishings for relaxation and comfort (Ex: no rugs; no soft furniture).

3.1 Enough furniture for routine care, play, and learning (Ex: each child has some place to store personal possessions; enough shelves for toys, books, and other materials).*

3.2 Almost all furniture is sturdy and in good repair (Ex: few if any problems, and none that cause a hazard).

3.3 Children with disabilities have the adaptive furniture that they need (Ex: child has special chair so he can join others at table; bars for stability in toilet area).
NA permitted

3.4 At least 2 soft furnishings are accessible to children during play.*

5.1 Ample furniture for routine care, play, and learning (Ex: children's possessions stored without items touching those of another child; children eat or work at tables without crowding; the vast majority of materials are not crowded on shelves).*

5.2 Chairs and tables are child-sized for 75% of the children (Ex: when sitting back in chair: feet touch floor, knees fit comfortably under table, table tops at about elbow height).

5.3 Two pieces of furniture, each designed for a different specific activity, used for that activity (Ex: easel for art; sand-water table; housekeeping furniture; wood-working bench).*

5.4 Furnishing(s) providing a substantial amount of softness accessible (Ex: mattress; upholstered child-sized couch; group of several large cushions).*

7.1 Routine care furniture is convenient to use (Ex: cubbies and cot/mats are easily accessible without leaving room).*

7.2 Three or more pieces of furniture designed for a specific activity are used.*

7.3 All furniture is clean and in good repair (Ex: no tears in soft furnishings that expose padding; all surfaces clean and well-maintained).

Notes for Clarification

1.1, 1.4, 3.1, 3.2, 3.4, 5.1, 5.2, 7.1, 7.2, 7.3. A "play area" is a space where play materials are provided for children to use. An "interest center" is a clearly defined play area for a particular kind of play. Materials are organized by type and stored so that they are accessible to the children. Furniture is provided for use of the materials, if needed. An appropriate amount of space is provided for the type of play being encouraged by the materials and the number of children allowed to play in the center. Since blocks and dramatic play materials are associated with more active play, interest centers for these materials should be larger than those for other materials, such as books, science, or fine motor. If the definition of "interest center" is not met, then credit can be given for the space being a "play area" only. "Interest centers" are a more specific, better designed type of play area.

3.3, 5.3. Note that this item is about room arrangement for play and learning, not for other issues. If there are difficulties with supervision because children leave the space as part of their play/learning (for example, going into the hall to run around or to play in other non-classroom spaces), consider this here. However, if children leave the room to use the toilet, consider any lack of supervision issues in Item 9, Toileting/diapering, or Item 11, Safety practices. If they leave for other reasons, such as going to cubbies or to bring something from another classroom, score in Item 11, Safety practices. This Indicator does not require that all children are visually supervised at all times. Adults may supervise through hearing children, as well as through seeing them. They must, however, know when serious problems occur and respond.

5.1. To score *Yes*, only a few minor problems can be observed, such as a child needing to walk through a narrow space where children are playing to get to another part of the room, but not disrupting the other children's play when doing so. It must be observed that use of a pathway disrupts play to score *No*.

5.2. A "cozy area" is a clearly defined space with a substantial amount of softness where children may lounge, daydream, read, or play quietly. For example, it might consist of a soft rug with several cushions, an upholstered couch, or a covered mattress with cushions. The cozy area must provide enough soft furnishings to allow a child to completely escape the normal hardness of the typical early childhood classroom. One *small* item, in itself, does not create a cozy area. For example, a small padded chair, small child-sized beanbag chair, a few small stuffed animals, or a carpeted corner, by themselves, are each not enough. However, credit could be given for a combination of such furnishings. Credit might be given for large furnishings, such as a mattress, couch, or adult-sized bean bag chair, if they provide the required amount of softness.

7.1. Noisy play areas include dramatic play, blocks, music instruments or music played without headphones, and active physical play. Quiet areas include books, writing, and listening centers for stories. Buffer centers, such as computer, science, fine motor, math, or art can be used to help separate the noisy centers from the quiet centers, but there should not be active, noisy play observed interfering with activities within the buffer centers. Separation by space, and not only by furniture, is required between noisy and quiet centers.

Inadequate		Minimal		Good		Excellent
1	2	3	4	5	6	7

3. Room arrangement for play and learning

1.1 Most play areas are so crowded that play cannot progress well.*

1.2 Very few play materials in classroom are organized for children's independent use.

1.3 Extremely difficult for teachers to supervise children while they play (Ex: many children frequently completely out of sight or hearing, and teachers do not circulate in room to monitor).

1.4 No play area is accessible for enrolled children with disabilities requiring special accommodation.*
NA permitted

3.1 At least 2 play areas have sufficient space for the type of play encouraged by the materials (Ex: chairs do not usually block access to materials on shelves; active areas have more space).*

3.2 At least 3 interest centers that meet the required definition are accessible.*

3.3 Teachers can minimally supervise children (Ex: can hear if there are problems and move to the area quickly; can see some of the children by glancing around the room).*

3.4 Some play areas are accessible to enrolled children with disabilities.*
NA permitted

5.1 Space is arranged so that classroom pathways generally do not interrupt play.*

5.2 At least 5 interest centers are used, **including a cozy area** protected from active play.*

5.3 Teachers can adequately supervise all children visually most of the time (Ex: if children are hidden, teachers move about the space often enough to ensure children's safety or to encourage learning).*

5.4 All play areas are accessible to enrolled children with disabilities.*
NA permitted

7.1 Quiet and noisy play areas are all separated from one another, not just by furniture but by physical space.*

7.2 All play areas requiring special provisions are conveniently equipped (Ex: art and sand/water interest centers have easily cleaned surfaces and sink near-by; block center has rug to reduce noise).*

7.3 Centers requiring more space (blocks, dramatic play, very popular or active play) have sufficient space to accommodate the type of play required and the number of children who want to participate.*

Note for Clarification

*The intent of a space for privacy is to give children relief from the pressures of group life. Isolation from the group as a punishment is not given credit in this Item. A place where 1 or 2 children can play protected from intrusion by others is considered a space for privacy. If 2 children use the space together, they must be able to select with whom they want to share the space. Do not count the computer or other "screen time" as the only space for privacy, since computer time should be strictly limited and time for using a space for privacy should not be. Do not count spaces that are designated for 1 or 2 children to use if they are in the midst of much activity. For example, do not count an easel in a busy art center, or a sand table designated for 2 children if it is located in a crowded or busy area of the room, where children using it are likely to be disturbed. Score supervision of the space(s) used for privacy in room arrangement, supervision, and safety-related items.

1.1, 3.1. Consider whether children may find a space where others are not interested in playing and then that space is considered an informal space for privacy, as long as there is a good chance that the child will not be interrupted by others. Consider both indoor and outdoor places where a child could have privacy.

1.2. If no child is intruded upon while using the space for privacy, assume that the system is in place and working well.

3.1. See definitions of "interest center" and "play area" under Explanation of Terms Used Throughout the Scale.

3.2, 5.3. If no problem is observed when children play alone or with a friend, give credit for this Indicator. Any intervention in problems must be done positively and the problem should not continue.

5.1. All "spaces where children play alone or with a friend" are not necessarily spaces set up specifically for that purpose. However, the space for privacy, as required in this Indicator, should be formally set up by staff to encourage 1 or 2 children to play without interruption. Such spaces are usually designated in an obvious manner—for example, by the number of chairs at a table, or by signs indicating that just 1 or 2 children are allowed in the area at a time.

5.3. If there is more than one space set up for privacy (meeting the requirement for 5.1), at least one must be consistently protected in order to give credit.

Inadequate		Minimal		Good		Excellent
1	2	3	4	5	6	7

4. Space for privacy*

1.1 Children not allowed to play alone or with a friend, indoors or outdoors (Ex: playing alone is unacceptable; children are kept in a group most of the day; outdoor play consists only of group exercises or games).*

1.2 No system or rule observed being used that protects children playing alone or with a friend (Ex: children forced to share toy they are engaged in using; children's individual play frequently interrupted by others).*

1.3 Staff observed not interacting, or interacting negatively, with the children who play alone or with a friend.

3.1 Children are allowed to play alone or with a friend, without interfering with other children's access to play areas or interest centers designed for more children.*

3.2 Staff always intervene if there are major problems in the space for privacy.*

5.1 An indoor space for privacy is accessible and physically set up in the classroom to discourage interruptions (Ex: easel for 1 child; writing table with 1 or 2 chairs; indoor beanbag toss game where only 2 children are allowed to play at one time).*

5.2 The space for privacy in 5.1 is accessible for 1 hour during the observation.

5.3 Staff generally protect children using space required in 5.1 from intrusion by others (Ex: children made aware of the rules for privacy; if intrusion occurs, staff stop and successfully prevent further interruption).*

7.1 Staff interact positively with children who play alone or with a friend, socially or to discuss ideas. *Observe twice*

7.2 Staff suggest that child move materials to the designated space for privacy when the child wants to work alone (Ex: child not forced to share, but encouraged to take toy to private space).

Notes for Clarification

*To be considered for this Item, display must be easily visible to the children. It must be located in the space used by the children most of the day (i.e., their classroom), and where they can easily see the content. Display that is placed up high must be large enough to see easily. Smaller, more detailed display, such as photos, must be placed down low so children can see the detail. Labels on shelves indicating where materials are to be stored or signs naming centers do not count as display.

1.3. One instance of staff talking to children about a displayed material must be observed to score *No.* Note the definition of "staff" in the Explanation of Terms Used Throughout the Scale.

1.3, 3.3, 5.4. "Talk about" means that staff use the content of the display to teach children. For example, staff might read print or name objects shown, explain displayed content, or ask questions about what is in the display.

3.2. A total of 2 pieces of artwork is required; not 2 per child enrolled. The artwork must be easy-to-find and obvious.

5.2, 7.1. Since the intent of this Item is to use display as a teaching tool that encourages vocabulary growth and increases children's knowledge base, to consider giving credit for these Indicators, the topics of interest in a classroom must change regularly, and evidence of this should be observed in the display and conversations around them. It should be obvious that the materials in the display are related to a theme, unit, or other topic of current interest on the day of the observation. Permanently displayed materials—such as a calendar, weather chart, and posters showing academic content such as the alphabet, colors, numbers, or shapes—are not considered for these Indicators. Look for evidence posted in activity plans, curriculum plans, etc.; in what is heard during the observation; and in the content of activities being done. If there are no obvious content areas discussed in the classroom that change periodically, then these Indicators must be scored *No.*

5.3. "Individualized" children's artwork means that each child has carried out the work in his or her own creative way. So individualized products will look quite different from one another. Even if a general subject is introduced by the staff and discussed with the children (e.g., things we see or like to do in Spring), as long as each child is encouraged to interpret and create his or her idea in his or her own way, then the resulting products will be unique and individualized. Projects where children follow a teacher's example and little individual creativity is allowed are not considered "individualized."

5. Child-related display*

1.1 No materials displayed for children.

1.2 Inappropriate materials for predominant age group are displayed (Ex: materials displayed in preschool classroom are intended for older, school-aged children; materials give a negative social message or show frightening images).

1.3 Staff do not talk about display with the children.*

3.1. Some appropriate materials, including photos of some children in the group, are displayed, and none are inappropriate (Ex: colorful posters; charts and graphs).

3.2 At least 2 pieces of children's artwork displayed.*

3.3 Staff talk about display materials at least once during the observation (Ex: discuss the calendar during circle time; point out a child's family photo; talk about who will do the classroom jobs; discuss weather chart).*

5.1 Many items displayed for children throughout the room.

5.2 Some of the display is related to topics of current interest to the children in the group (Ex: pictures related to current topic of discussion; seasonal pictures; photos of events children participated in).*

5.3 About one-third of the display materials are children's individualized artwork.*

5.4 Staff talk about display materials at least two different times during free play and/or routines in a way that interests the children.*

7.1 About half of the display is related to current interests of children in the group, and one can easily tell what children's interests are, or what they are discussing.*

7.2 Staff use display to encourage informal conversations with the children.
Observe once

7.3 Staff are observed pointing out and reading the words in the display in a way that interests the children.

7.4 Three-dimensional child-created work is displayed, in addition to flat work.

Notes for Clarification

*Observe any on-site space(s) regularly used by the children for gross motor activity. Include indoor and outdoor spaces used, based on weather or other conditions. For example, when weather does not permit use of outdoor space, an indoor space might be used. This may have to be done after the 3-hour observation has been completed. Base score on the assessment of the gross motor space(s) normally used for the children, even if on-site gross motor space(s) was not used on the day of the observation. Gross motor safety information is available at www.ersi.info. Look under the Supplementary Materials for the scales. Apply the safety standards to regularly-used indoor and outdoor spaces.

1.3. Score *Yes* if gross motor space is used for less than 10 minutes of the observation in a program of any length.

1.2, 3.2, 5.3. When considering safety hazards, do not try to imagine every possible accident that could occur, and do not consider all hazards to be an equal threat. Use guidance from the Consumer Product Safety Commission's *Public Playground Safety Handbook* when determining the safety problems in gross motor spaces. When scoring, consider the characteristics of the whole space; not just the hazards observed in any part of the space.

"Minor hazards" have a low risk of causing serious injury, while "major hazards" have a high risk. Major hazards, such as a lack of fall zones, are given more power when considering the score for these indicators. Minor hazards mean that there is a danger, but it is unlikely to cause a problem, such as protrusions on fences that children do not show interest in, tree roots present but not likely to cause a fall onto a very hard surface, or fall zones that miss the required cushioning depth by only 1 or 2 inches. "Generally safe" (5.3) means that there are no major hazards, with appropriate fall zones, appropriate fences, and no other extreme problems. It is unlikely that children will be seriously injured in a generally safe space, although there may be some minor hazards.

"Extremely dangerous" (1.2) means that there are many major hazards in areas where children usually play. For example, there is no fence and no fall zone under high climbing equipment. "Somewhat safe" means that the safety of the space is about midway between "extremely dangerous" and "generally safe" (no major hazards). Therefore, "somewhat safe" means that there is adequate safe space to play, even if all the space is not hazard-free, and some attempt has been made to reduce major safety hazards (such as providing some cushioning under equipment), even if one or two serious hazards may still be present, but there is plenty of hazard-free play space used by the children. Any major hazards are not located in the areas where children play most of the time.

3.1. An "adequate" outdoor space must be large enough to allow all children using it to run freely. The space should be used for at least 15 minutes during the observation in a program of any length (weather permitting for outdoor space). If weather does not permit use of outdoor space, some indoor space must be used for the required 15 minutes of the observation. This indoor space may be too limited to allow free running, but it must still allow for gross motor activity, such as vigorous exercise or dancing, without children being crowded.

5.1. In order to give credit, both the outdoor and indoor spaces do not need to be used, as long as one of the spaces is used. For this indicator, any space used regularly must be large enough to accommodate children's free running. The presence of wheel toys is not required, but the space for use allows that they could be added. At this level of quality, a crowded circle time space is not considered spacious enough to be given credit.

5.2. If space cannot be used outdoors because of bad weather, then an adequate indoor space must be observed being used. For programs of less than 3 hours, at least 20 minutes is required during the observation.

5.4. If children have to walk through hazardous areas, such as parking lots, crossing streets, or use a long flight of stairs, then score this indicator *No*, but do not count these hazards when determining the safety of the gross motor space observed. Consider such hazards and the extent to which they are supervised in Item 11, Safety practices.

7.1. Fall zone surfaces cannot count as one of the two surfaces.

6. Space for gross motor play*

1.1 No outdoor or indoor space is used for gross motor play.

1.2 Observed gross motor space is extremely dangerous (Ex: parking lot for cars also used for play; completely unfenced area; no fall zones for high equipment).*

1.3 Space for gross motor activity is used for less than 10 minutes during the observation.*

3.1 At least 1 adequate gross motor space, either outdoors or indoors, is used for at least 15 minutes.*

3.2 Gross motor area is somewhat safe (Ex: area for running has no major hazards such as much broken glass, deep holes; some attempt to provide fall zones; area fenced and gates kept closed).*

5.1 Observed gross motor space(s) spacious enough to allow vigorous play, including running and use of wheel toys.*

5.2 Gross motor space(s) used for at least 30 minutes.*

5.3 Gross motor area(s) generally safe, with no more than 4 minor hazards and no major hazards (Ex: low climber has 8 inches instead of 9 inches of loose protective cushioning; fence has protrusions in areas where causing a problem is unlikely; bollards not provided but area is far from quiet street).*

5.4 Gross motor space(s) easily accessible to the children (Ex: does not require a long walk, going through other classrooms, or use of stairs to access).*

7.1 Observed gross motor space(s) has at least 2 types of play surfaces, 1 hard and 1 soft, so that different types of activities are possible.*

7.2 Space(s) has at least 2 convenient features (Ex: outdoor protection from the elements, such as shade, good drainage; water fountain; close to toilets; accessible storage for portable equipment; direct access from classroom).

7.3 Space(s) arranged and used so that different activities do not interfere with one another (Ex: play with wheel toys separated from climbing equipment and ball play).

Notes for Clarification

*Observe any on-site stationary equipment used by the children to determine appropriateness, even if it is not used during the observation. Consider both portable and stationary equipment observed being used. "Stationary equipment" is not moved by the children as part of their play. For example, climbing structures, basketball hoops, and balance beams are considered stationary, even if they may be moveable by an adult or not anchored to the ground. "Portable gross motor equipment" is anything that the child moves as a part of gross motor play, including wheel toys, jump ropes, balls, and hula hoops. When considering the time children are given to use equipment, a small absence from access is not considered, such as when a child needs to leave the area to use the toilet or to get a drink of water. However, children should not have to spend long periods without access. For example, if a small group of children is taken to use the toilet and this takes up a substantial amount of the time required to access materials, do not give credit, even if other children are able to have access for the full time.

1.1 *No.* If any gross motor equipment is used either indoors or outdoors, score 1.1 *No.* To be considered appropriate, the gross motor equipment must be safe for the children, and suited to their age and ability.

1.3. If less than 10 minutes of access to the equipment is provided during the observation, score *Yes* in programs of any length.

3.1. In programs of any length, a minimum of 15 minutes of access is required to score *Yes.*

3.2, 5.2. According to the Consumer Product Safety Commission's *Public Playground Safety Handbook,* equipment such as trampolines, climbing ropes not secured at both ends, animal figure swings, multiple occupancy swings, rope swings, dual-exercise rings, and trapeze bars are considered "extremely dangerous." For preschool-aged children, and should not be used. Access the handout "Playground Information to Use with the Environment Rating Scales" at www.ersi.info. It is suggested that the handout be printed and taped into the scale. To determine whether half of the equipment is appropriate, consider the various components of a complex climber, such as access and exit areas, bridges, steps to the various platforms, and count each section separately. For example, if most of a climber is appropriate, but one platform is too high for the children, consider the platform as only one part of all the other components of the equipment.

3.3. The requirement of "7 different skills," requires different types of equipment. Generally, 1 piece of equipment will not provide the variety needed, but in the case of a very complex climber the indicator might be true. Other skills, besides those listed in the example, might include pulling/pushing, hanging by arms (for 4+-year-olds only), swinging, jumping, hopping, using a jump rope or a hula hoop, tossing things into containers, catching, throwing, or kicking. Observe to see how many skills the equipment encourages and list them. Consider both portable and stationary equipment. For balls, list 2 skills (e.g., catching, throwing, or kicking) as appropriate, but do not attribute more skills unless other equipment is added, such as a bat or a basketball hoop. For tricycles, list 2 skills of pedaling and steering. Do not count skills that are not stimulated by equipment, such as running, hopping, or skipping across the ground.

5.3. For programs of less than 3 hours, 20 minutes of access to gross motor equipment is required.

7.2. At this level, safety helmets are required for children using any wheel toys. The helmets must be properly supervised, fit each child well, and removed when use of the wheel toy is finished. Children should not be observed running or using other equipment wearing safety helmets. If helmets are used while children are on climbing equipment, count as a major safety hazard due to the danger of strangulation if caught on equipment in other areas of playground.

7. Gross motor equipment*

1.1 Very little or no gross motor equipment used both indoors and outdoors (Ex: children rarely get a turn, or have to wait long periods of time before getting a turn; equipment is very crowded, with no alternatives).*

1.2 Most of the equipment is not appropriate for the age and ability of the children (Ex: slides and climbers that are too high for preschooler; toddler-sized riding toys and climbers that do not challenge preschoolers; balls deflated).

1.3 Equipment is used for less than 10 minutes during the observation.*

3.1 Some gross motor equipment is used by the children for at least 15 minutes of the observation (Ex: each child has a reasonable chance to use the available equipment, without long waits).*

3.2 At least half of the accessible equipment (both portable and stationary) is appropriate for the age and ability of the children, and no equipment that could be considered "extremely dangerous" is ever used.*

3.3 Equipment stimulates at least 7 different skills.*

5.1 There is enough equipment (stationary and portable) to interest all of the children and keep them active and involved.

5.2 Almost all of the equipment credited in 5.1 is appropriate for the age and ability of the children.*

5.3 Equipment is accessible to the children for at least 30 minutes during the observation.*

5.4 Adaptations are made or special equipment provided for children with disabilities in the group who require them.
NA permitted

7.1 Use of ample and varied equipment is observed, indoors or outdoors (Ex: no waiting to use popular equipment; climbers not crowded; enough balls; different skills encouraged by equipment).

7.2 All observed equipment, including use of safety helmets, is appropriate for the children's age and ability.*

7.3 Equipment is provided to encourage more advanced age-appropriate skills (Ex: plastic baseballs and bats; child-sized golf clubs, balls and "holes"; long-jump challenge; bicycle with training wheels).

28

Notes for Clarification

1.2, 3.3, 5.3, 7.1. Since 3 important health practices are required (washing/sanitizing the eating surface, hand hygiene before and after eating, and serving uncontaminated foods), consider the extent to which each of these required health practices is followed. If there is little effort in 2 of the 3 health practices (for example, handwashing is completely ignored, there is no attempt to clean tables, and/or foods are served under conditions that cause extreme contamination), then score 1.2 *Yes.* There can be minor lapses in following the handwashing procedure (not rubbing for the 20 seconds, but rubbing all hand surfaces thoroughly; not wetting hands first but soap still makes bubbles). However, hands should be cleaned reasonably well. If there is a significant attempt to complete all practices, even if some procedures are not done absolutely correctly, score 3.3. *Yes.* If there is a minimal attempt to do all procedures, but the practices are completed with many serious errors, score 3.3 *No.* When a flexible snack time is provided, and children come and go throughout a period of time, the same sanitary conditions are required, such as sanitizing the table between use by different children, handwashing completed. If children use hands to eat, handwashing is required after eating to remove saliva and food.

3.1. Sometimes young children are so involved in their play that they may ignore their food needs. Therefore, if a meal or snack is offered as a choice to children (e.g., during free play time), some system must be in place to ensure that children come to the snack area or table, see foods being offered, and choose whether or not they want to eat. This option of choosing whether to participate in a snack should be offered only to older preschoolers. Occasionally, children have been provided with a meal or snack just prior to arriving at the program, so that they are not hungry for the meal/snack being served. These children can be exempt from eating if they are shown the meal/snack and make the decision to not eat, and do not have to be fed until the next regularly scheduled meal/snack.

3.2. To score *Yes*, at least 75% of the children must have the components required for the meal or snack observed.

5.2. When children are given choices about what to eat/drink, all children should be clearly offered all components so that they can make an informed choice about what to eat/drink. For children with allergies or family preferences, the appropriate substitutions must be offered (e.g., soy or rice milk for regular milk; soy substitute for meat; apple for citrus fruit). Credit can be given for serving all components at the same time as long as children were clearly offered all components, even if they did not select all.

5.4. Older groups of children should be observed taking more responsibility than younger groups of children. For example, 4-year-olds would be expected to help more with serving or setting the table, rather than simply clearing their places, which might be expected of younger children. Children should be supervised in their efforts by teachers who ensure that procedures are followed correctly, and child-sized utensils and pitchers should be provided when needed.

PERSONAL CARE ROUTINES

8. Meals/snacks

1.1 Food served is of unacceptable nutritional value (Ex: USDA standards not usually followed; food from home not supplemented as needed).

1.2 Very little attempt to meet sanitary requirements.*

1.3 Negative atmosphere (Ex: long periods of waiting; punitive emphasis on manners and proper behavior; quiz children rather than having friendly conversations; inappropriate expectations for developmental abilities).

3.1 Schedule is appropriate for children (Ex: no child goes for more than 3 hours without eating, unless asleep or just ate before arriving at the program; children offered or can get water when thirsty; if snack offered at free choice time, staff encourage each child to participate).*

3.2 Food is of appropriate nutritional value for most children. (Ex: meets USDA guidelines; food provided by parents supplemented as needed; appropriate substitutes provided for children with allergies or family dietary preferences).*

3.3 Some attempts made to meet sanitary requirements (Ex: tables are cleaned in some way; children and adults attempt hand hygiene, even if not according to required procedure; foods served on plates and not on tabletop).*

5.1 Schedule allows for flexibility (Ex: children who finish are allowed to go to another activity; snack schedule allows children some choice about when to eat; child who arrives late offered breakfast).

5.2 All required components of the meal/snack are served together (Ex: milk offered with solid foods, not after; healthful fruits offered with other foods).*

5.3 Proper sanitary requirements usually followed (Ex: most children and staff use hand hygiene properly; tables are usually washed and sanitized according to procedure).*

5.4 Children encouraged to help during meals and snacks, with staff supervision and instruction as needed (Ex: set table; serve themselves with child-sized utensils; clear table; wipe up spills; manage own snack brought from home).*

5.5 Some staff-child or child-child conversations at meals/snacks.

7.1 Sanitary procedures are met almost all of the time, with only a few minor lapses.*

7.2 Atmosphere is relaxed with many conversations and pleasant social interaction (Ex: staff are pleasant and helpful; children eat in small groups, rather than in one large group; room is not noisy or crowded; staff sit with children and model pleasant interaction).

7.3 Staff actively teach self-help skills as children are ready (Ex: teach child to use napkin and spoon; teach 3's to use forks, and give safe knives to older preschoolers to learn to cut).

Notes for Clarification

1.2, 3.3, 5.2, 7.2. Basic sanitary procedures for diapering/toileting include hand hygiene, flushing toilets, keeping diapering/toileting sinks separate from sinks used for other purposes or sanitizing sinks used for multiple purposes that include diapering/toileting, and maintaining sanitary conditions in the area, such as by cleaning up spills, keeping diapering area clean and disinfected. When scoring, consider all procedures together, and decide whether almost no attempt was made to carry out the procedures (1.2), a medium attempt was made, but there were many lapses in doing the requirements (3.3), much effort was made but parts of the procedure were not correct (5.2), or the procedures were completely carried out with few if any lapses (7.2).

1.3, 3.4. To score 3.4 *Yes*, staff do not completely ignore children using the toilet, and appear to know where the children are, pay some attention to every child using the toileting area, at least during part of the procedure. Staff may pay intermittent attention when actively watching children. When children use a toilet in the classroom space, and are completely unsupervised with no staff nearby, give credit if *all* children observed using the toilet with little or no supervision complete the whole procedure correctly, including proper use of toilet, wiping as needed, flushing, hand hygiene, and managing clothes. If it is impossible to tell whether the child follows the proper procedures, usually because the door is closed and the child is not visible, score based on the extent to which the staff supervise children using the toilet. If they cannot see into the toileting area, but talk through the door to check on the child, and then can see whether the child washed hands in the classroom sink, base the score on what is observed, in terms of completeness of the visible procedure and the extent to which the teacher checks on the children. When children use the toilet in a completely unsupervised toileting area, even within the classroom, and staff pay no attention at all, score indicator 1.3 *Yes*. In those programs where children leave the classroom for toileting because the toilet area used is located in a space separate from the classroom, for example, down the hallway or in another classroom, all children using the toilet must be accompanied by a staff member.

3.1. If no child is observed using the toilet during the observation, and there is no staff reminder to encourage any child to use the toilet, score *No*.

3.4, 5.3. If children carry out the toileting procedure, including proper use of the toilet (wiping as needed, flushing, etc.), handwashing correctly, and behave in a responsible manner when toileting, supervision of each child is not required to score *Yes*.

7.1. "Convenient" means that the toileting area is adjacent to or in the same space as the classroom.

9. Toileting/diapering

1.1 Basic provisions are generally lacking (Ex: no towels, toilet paper, or soap within reach; no running water in toileting/diapering area; toilets very difficult to access, require a long walk).

1.2 Very little attempt to complete basic sanitary procedures (Ex: almost nothing is done to ensure sanitary conditions; proper hand sanitizing or handwashing rarely used; toilets rarely flushed or checked; contaminated sink not disinfected; accidents not cleaned up).*

1.3 Staff generally do not pay attention to children involved in toileting/diapering procedures *or* supervision is unpleasant (Ex: children go down hall to use toilet unattended; closed doors where staff cannot see or hear children; staff handle children roughly, yell at them).*

3.1 Toileting schedule meets basic needs of all children (Ex: no accidents observed; diapers or pull-ups checked and changed at least once during the observation; group toileting times cause no problems).*

3.2 Basic provisions are usually accessible for use during children's toileting/diapering (Ex: soap, toilet paper within reach; if something is missing, staff quickly replace it).

3.3 Some attempts to meet sanitary requirements (toilets usually flushed; pull-ups changed with some sanitary precautions; children and staff attempt hand hygiene even if not correct procedure).*

3.4 Staff provide some supervision (Ex: staff can hear and talk to child in stall although they cannot supervise visually; handwashing is supervised but not the children who are using toilet stalls; children never leave room to use toilet alone).*

5.1 Toileting schedule is individualized (Ex: children can use toilet when they need to; changing diapers/pull-ups checked and changed every 2 hours; children playing outdoors can be taken to toilet with no problem).

5.2 Proper sanitary requirements generally followed (Ex: most children and staff use hand hygiene properly; sinks disinfected as needed).*

5.3 Supervision is pleasant and ensures that children carry out toileting/diapering procedures correctly (Ex: careful teaching of self-help skills; pictured steps to handwashing pointed out; children watched closely).*

7.1 Convenient, easily supervised toileting area with child-sized toilet and sink allows children to use as needed.*

7.2 Sanitary procedures are met almost all of the time, with only a few minor lapses.*

7.3 Staff are responsive to children's individual personalities and needs (Ex: remind children who need to use toilet; are patient and supportive with child who is fearful; balance privacy with the need to supervise).

Notes for Clarification

*This item addresses additional times when handwashing is required, other than those covered in Item 8, Meals/snacks and Item 9, Toileting/diapering. There are 5 categories of handwashing that must be tracked to score this indicator: (1) Upon arrival into classroom, and re-entering classroom after being outside; (2) Before and after shared use of wet materials, such as play dough or water; (3) After play with shared sensory materials, such as sand, or after messy play; (4) After dealing with bodily fluids; and (5) After touching contaminated objects and surfaces. To score, observers should be aware of times that handwashing is carried out when needed. In addition, other procedures to protect children's health, such as sanitary nap provision, nonsmoking policy in center, and staff modeling good health practices are included.

1.1. For example, no attempt to have children/staff use hand hygiene when they arrive and re-enter the class from outdoor play; runny noses ignored and not wiped; animal contamination visible in outdoor or indoor area where children play with no attempt to remove it; staff ignore children's access to contaminated objects that have been discarded. If children consistently and independently complete most hygienic procedures correctly, with no staff input, score *No* since it is obvious that children have been taught to do so.

1.2, 3.2, 5.2. If no evidence relating to nap is observed, or the program does not provide nap, score these indicators *NA*. If no naptime is observed, score 5.2 *NA*. Even if naptime is not observed, score indicators 1.2 and 3.2 based on any evidence of problems found. For example, children's bedding might be observed stored in a pile without separation; many cots/mats are stored so that they are contaminated. When scoring, consider all sanitary procedures and base score on the amount done correctly. In considering observed nap, individual cots, mats, and bedding should be stored so that they do not touch; an attempt must be made to place all cots/mats at least 36 inches apart; putting children who are less than 36 inches apart alternating head to foot so children are not breathing in one another's faces; using barriers when cots/mats cannot be placed 36 inches apart, and no child uses soft furnishings for nap that are used by other children for play and learning. Much compliance with these requirements is expected in 5.2, with only minor lapses, such as a barrier used between only two cots, or the stored linens of two children were observed touching a little, but the other linens were not touching.

5.1. If children consistently and independently complete most hygiene procedures correctly, with no staff input, score *Yes* since it is obvious that children have been taught to do so.

5.3. Some staff lapses are acceptable, but generally they should be good models.

7.2. Do not give credit if children carry out health practices incorrectly because this means that they are not ready to do the tasks independently. Examples of encouraging health practices include children taught handwashing song to guide proper procedure; praised when they use a tissue to wipe their nose, discard it, and wash their hands; younger child is praised for putting on own coat or helping another child to do so.

7.3. Do not give credit if displayed materials do not show correct procedure or if they are not used/followed when children carry out the tasks. To give credit, the displayed materials must be easily seen by the children.

10. Health practices*

1.1 Little attention paid to children's health practices.*

1.2 Little attempt to ensure that nap/rest provisions are sanitary.*
NA permitted

1.3 Smoking occurs either in the indoor or outdoor areas used by the children or children have access to smoke related debris (Ex: cigarette butts; second-hand smoke easily detectable).

3.1 Some attention paid to children's health practices (Ex: reminding children to wash hands or use hand sanitizer; stopping child from drinking water from water play table; wiping nose and disposing of tissue properly).

3.2 Some attempt made to practice sanitary nap procedures (Ex: children have sheets on the sleeping surface; most cots are at least 18 inches apart, and none are very close together).*
NA permitted

3.3 Staff are positive with the children as they carry out hygiene tasks.

5.1 Staff usually help children learn to carry out hygiene practices correctly (Ex: hands washed upon arrival and at other times when needed; sing handwashing song).*

5.2 Staff carry out sanitary nap procedures with only a few lapses.*
NA permitted

5.3 Staff are generally good models of health practices (Ex: eat healthy foods in front of children; avoid standing while eating or drinking; show enthusiasm for physical activity and going outside; use handwashing procedure correctly).*

7.1 Proper sanitary procedures used consistently as needed, with few lapses.

7.2 Children are encouraged to manage health practices as independently as they are able, and staff continue to guide the children who still need more help.*

7.3 Picture/word reminders/instructions of required health practices are displayed and used with the children when needed to teach sanitary practices, such as handwashing, toothbrushing, or wiping nose.*

Notes for Clarification

*To score, use guidance from the Consumer Product Safety Commission's *Public Playground Safety Handbook*, *Caring for Our Children*, and the ASTM guidelines as needed, but still consider whether in the specific circumstances, problems are major. Gross motor safety information used to score is available at www.ersi.info. Look under the Supplementary Materials for the scales.

1.1, 1.2, 3.1, 3.2, 5.1, 7.1. No stimulating environment can be completely safe for young children. Therefore, the intent of this item, and others where safety is a consideration, is to lower risk of injury to children by minimizing hazards and providing appropriate supervision for the age and ability of children in the group. During the observation, both indoor and outdoor safety hazards are considered. Not all hazards are given the same weight in scoring, however. A major safety hazard is one where the risk of serious injury is very high. A minor hazard is either one where the consequences would not be as great, or the accident would be less likely, due for example to the nature of the supervision, the characteristics of the children in the group, or the amount of exposure to the hazard. When noting hazards, do not try to imagine every possible accident that could occur. Instead, consider the seriousness of the hazard and how likely it is to happen. Here are some examples of major hazards compared to minor hazards:

- An uncovered outlet is located within reach, close to the water table where children are playing on a wet floor, compared to an uncovered outlet that is not within children's reach or not in a place where it is likely to cause a problem.
- A bottle of full-strength bleach is left within reach where children are playing or eating, compared to a bottle that is stored up high, out of reach, but not locked.

- A low climber has no fall zone and is located on cement, compared to the same climber with a fall zone that has almost enough cushioning to meet the Consumer Product Safety Commission's requirement for cushioning.
- A playground fence is not protected by bollards from traffic on a very busy street with speeding cars, compared to a small part of a fence being unprotected on a similar street.
- An entrapment hazard on frequently used piece of playground equipment, compared to the same type of hazard located between the gate and fence, in a place where it is much less likely to cause a problem.
- Exposed tree roots located where children usually run, and tripping would result in a fall onto a cement surface, compared to tree roots on a soft surface where children rarely run.

1.1, 3.1. Observe any on-site outdoor spaces/stationary equipment regularly used to determine safety. If the space/equipment is not used during the 3-hour observation, observe before or after the observation is completed. Score NA if no on-site outdoor space is used by the program. This may include non-gross motor space used, for example, for science, art, or other non-gross motor activities.

3.3. "Some supervision" will depend on whether the supervision is related to major or minor safety issues. However, in general, "some" indicates that the supervision is about halfway between what would be found in 1.3 (grossly inadequate) and in 5.3 (always stop dangerous behavior).

5.3. Staff should stop all behavior that is likely to cause major problems. It is impossible for staff to stop any and all behavior that could possibly cause minor injuries, or that has a minimal risk.

Inadequate		Minimal		Good		Excellent
1	2	3	4	5	6	7

11. Safety practices*

1.1 Many major hazards that carry a high risk of serious injury to children are present in the outdoor environment.*
NA permitted

1.2 Many major hazards that carry a high risk of serious injury to children are present in the indoor environment.*

1.3 Supervision is grossly inadequate during much of the observation, so children's safety is not protected both indoors and outdoors (Ex: staff do not go outside with children; no staff in room for longer than a momentary lapse).

1.4 Staff encourage obviously dangerous behavior in children (Ex: child challenged to jump from high equipment or climber; carry bowl of hot soup or sharp knife back to kitchen; hurry on stairs; play dangerous chasing game).

3.1 No more than 3 major hazards that carry a high risk of serious injury to children are present in the outdoor environment.*
NA permitted

3.2 No more than 3 major hazards that carry a high risk of serious injury to children are present in the indoor environment.*

3.3 Some supervision to stop major safety problems provided both outdoors and indoors (Ex: staff are always in the same space as the children, can usually see or hear them; consider ages and abilities of children; stop the most obvious dangerous behavior).*

3.4 Staff never observed encouraging obviously dangerous behavior in children.

5.1 No more than 2 major safety hazards are present, outdoors or indoors.*

5.2 Staff usually anticipate and take action to prevent safety problems (Ex: remove toys from fall zones; close gates or doors as needed; sweep sand off of running area; wipe up spills that make floors slippery).

5.3 Staff always stop potentially dangerous behavior in children.*

7.1 No major safety hazards are present outdoors or indoors, and only a few minor hazards observed.*

7.2 Each staff member usually attends to an area of responsibility, while remaining aware of the entire space, and responding as other staff and children move, in order to ensure appropriate supervision in the entire area.

7.3 Staff generally adjust supervision based on relative risks and the characteristics of children in the group (Ex: give more attention to impulsive child who tends to put self in danger; spends more time closely supervising the more dangerous equipment).

Notes for Clarification

*In scoring, consider only the staff who are usually in the classroom working with the children. For the definition of "staff", see Explanation of Terms Used Throughout the Scale. Exposure to adult language is a necessity for children's positive language development. Therefore, to give credit for any Indicator, all children should generally be well exposed to what is required. If there are long periods with little or no exposure to language from the staff, such as a lack of staff circulation among children during free play, do not give credit. There should be some language experiences for children during gross motor times, but less is expected than during other times for play or routines. Consider the language used by all staff usually in the classroom when scoring. To give credit, requirements should represent regular practice.

1.1, 3.2, 5.1. In determining whether the language used meets the requirements, ask yourself if you can tell what staff are referring to or talking about just by listening and not looking. Note numbers of different words staff use with the children throughout the observation, not just at one time. Descriptive words (adjectives and adverbs) add meaning or specificity to words for people, places, things (nouns), or actions (verbs). They include color, size, and shape words, and many others, such as "pretty", "comfortable", "slowly", "exciting", or "huge".

1.3, 3.3, 5.3. For these Indicators, look for how often staff talk about the materials, toys, and display materials indoors and outdoors, helping children tie the words to what they refer to. For 1.3, there would be very little or no talk in which staff name things, describe them, or bring up new ideas. Children playing would be ignored in terms of staff talking to them about their play. There would be little if any talk about things in the room during group times or routines. To score 5.3 Yes, you would observe many words being used very often while children play with toys during free play, and also as children participate in routines and group times. There would be obvious attention to children's language during the vast majority of times. Note that Indicator 5.3 requires ample materials to talk about, and increased opportunities for staff to use a wider variety of words with children in a meaningful way. Indicator 3.3 represents the midpoint between 1.3 and 5.3, with sporadic use of words related to the things in the room. There might be times when no words are used, and times when they are.

5.1. To score Yes, this must be observed to be the usual practice, happening frequently.

5.2. In scoring this Indicator, listen for staff answering children's questions about what a word means or using an unfamiliar word and providing the definition.

5.4. Score NA if there is no child with an obvious special language need. Language used during non–"whole-group" times is more likely to meet individual needs.

For children with language disabilities, the teaching of vocabulary should be based on what the child experiences in the "here and now," and if special methods are helpful, such as signing, these should be observed. Children whose family language differs from that spoken in the program should be handled with more exactness in what is said, and more clues provided for understanding.

7.1. To give credit, staff should be observed using less common words in their talk. For example, staff might use words for feelings, such as "disappointed", "anxious", "delighted", instead of only "happy" or "sad"; or for actions, words might include "speedy", "instantaneous" instead of "fast" and "slow"; instead of saying "fish" for the fish in the aquarium, staff might add the type of fish, such as "guppy" or "beta". Instead of saying "green", staff use the more specific shade words, such as "turquoise" or "light green".

7.2. The provision of new themes or topics to discuss should be obvious to the observer, and should go well beyond talking about letter, color, number, or days of the week, even though such topics might be used to introduce some new words. It is expected that the themes or topics (either initiated by staff or by children) would provide a rich environment for new experiences that children can use to increase understanding of what they already know, expand their knowledge base, and increase vocabulary.

7.3. "Staff add information and ideas" should be differentiated from staff asking questions to get children to say more (credited in the next item. Encouraging children to use language). To "expand children's understanding" means that staff respond verbally to what a child has said, and carry the child's idea further, providing additional information and vocabulary that the child can attach to the meaning of what she or he said. For example, if a 4-year-old says, "I have a truck," the teacher might expand on the idea of "truck" by responding with, "It is a dump truck. This truck carries heavy loads here in the back section. It can carefully to the load when the back part goes up and the load falls out." Frequently, you will hear them repeat the word ("I see the truck") or ask a question. Sometimes they will add a very short amount of information (child says "truck," and the teacher responds "a red truck", "I like trucks"). However, at this level of quality the staff response should be more extensive ("Trucks come in many sizes. I have a small pick-up truck. You've seen it in the parking lot. But there are also very big trucks that are used to carry freight. Some of the big trucks even have a place for the driver to sleep in a bed."). Besides statements made by a child, expansions may be heard as staff respond to questions children ask by providing substantial related information.

LANGUAGE AND LITERACY

12. Helping children expand vocabulary*

1.1 Staff use very limited vocabulary with the children (Ex: specific names for objects and actions rarely used; few descriptive words used; "this," "that," "it," used in place of more exact words).*

1.2 Staff teaching of words is not related to children's actual experience (Ex: calendar used to teach days of the week, but days of the week not used in conversations about when things happen; weather words used when doing weather chart, but not when children actually experience weather).

1.3 Staff do not use the opportunities provided by classroom materials, display, or other concrete experiences to introduce words.*

3.1 Staff sometimes use the names for people, places, things, and actions as children experience them in routines or play, throughout the observation (Ex: name foods for lunch, name the objects children use and actions they take).*

3.2 Words that describe people, places, things, and actions are sometimes used within a meaningful context for the children (Ex: "You're wearing a *soft blue* shirt." "Today we are having *square* crackers." "You are walking so *quietly*.").*

3.3 Staff sometimes use the opportunities provided by classroom materials, display, or other concrete experiences to introduce words.*

5.1 Staff frequently use specific words for people, places, things, actions, and descriptive words as children experience routines and play.*

5.2 Staff sometimes correctly explain the meaning of unfamiliar words in a way children can understand (Ex: "Fog is really tiny bits of water and that is why it feels wet."; "When I say that I am concerned, it means that I care what happens to you.").*
Observe twice

5.3 Staff frequently use the opportunities provided by materials, display, activities, or other meaningful experiences to introduce words.*

5.4 Special accommodations are observed for children to suit their diagnosed disabilities or family language needs (Ex: demonstrates with hands the meaning of words; says words in two languages; uses a language board or computer technology; uses signing with speech).*
NA permitted

7.1 Staff generally use a wide range of words to specify more exactly what they are talking about, appropriate to ages and abilities of the children.*

7.2 Staff introduce new themes or topics of interest to provide a wide and interesting range of new words.*

7.3 Staff add information and ideas in order to expand children's understanding of the meaning of words children use.*
Observe twice

Consider how staff communicate with all children when scoring, and how much language is used under circumstances where individualizing is possible. Language used during non–whole-group times will be more likely to meet individual needs. See if staff challenge more developmentally advanced children to use more complex language and longer sentences, and to take more turns in conversations, while challenging children with less ability to talk at their own level of ability and comfort. For children with far less language ability (or who speak a family language that differs from that used in the program), staff should encourage children to name objects and actions and use short sentences about what they are experiencing in the "here and now." Preschoolers with more advanced language should be asked more questions requiring longer answers, while less advanced children should be asked simpler questions.

5.1. These frequently asked questions might require shorter or longer answers, as long as children show interest and enjoyment in answering.

5.4. To give credit, staff should be observed asking children to talk to one another, or initiating a conversation in which more than 1 child in engaged, all contributing in some way that goes beyond simply listening to another child talking to an adult.

7.1. These frequently asked questions should include many that elicit longer answers from the children.

7.2. If no gross motor free play is observed, score based on what is observed during routines.

Notes for Clarification

*In scoring, consider only the staff who are usually in the classroom working with the children. For the definition of "staff", see Explanation of Terms Used Throughout the Scale.

1.2, 3.2, 7.2. Staff should respond when they are addressed or approached by the children. Look for instances when children are trying to show or tell something to a staff member to see whether they are ignored or responded to. Staff must be close enough and show interest and positive responsiveness to encourage a child to initiate communication. If staff tend to remain separate from many of the children during free play times, or children do not usually initiate communication with the staff, credit is not given for 7.2.

1.3, 3.3, 5.2, 7.2, 7.3. In order to give credit for *conversation*, there must be some talking between a staff member and an individual child, or a small group of children, one listening, the other communicating either verbally or nonverbally. There must also be a common topic or interest for the conversation, something both staff and child are mutually attending to. The conversation may be initiated by either the staff or the child, but both staff and child must take turns for the interaction to be considered a conversation. In cases where children are less verbal, the conversation may be shorter and include responses from the children in gestures, or sign language may be used by both parties, if needed. Do not count staff asking simple one-word-answer questions, such as asking a child to name an item or to tell its color.

1.4, 3.4, 5.3. In any group of children with a typical range of ages, there will be children of differing language needs, some more obvious than others.

13. Encouraging children to use language*

1.1 The majority of questions staff ask children require rote or yes/no answers that children have difficulty answering correctly (Ex: "What color is this?" "What shape is this?")

1.2 Staff ignore much of what children say, respond to their talk negatively, or do not respond appropriately.*

1.3 Few staff-child conversations where each child takes turns according to ability.*

1.4 Staff make no attempt to encourage children to communicate (Ex: no singing, nursery rhymes, saying alphabet, naming colors).*

1.5 Social environment does not encourage much talking among children or with staff (Ex: strict atmosphere where child talk not encouraged; little time to interact socially).

3.1 Staff ask occasional "non-rote" questions that children can answer successfully (Ex: "Where did you get your new shoes?" "Do you like to eat this cheese?" "What do you see in the picture?")

3.2 Staff pay moderate amount of attention to what children say, responding either neutrally or positively, but not negatively.*

3.3 Some staff-child conversations observed intermittently.*

3.4 Some attempts to maximize children's individual abilities to communicate (Ex: attempt to understand what less verbal child is trying to say; waits for response from child; understands a few words in child's family language or in sign language).*

3.5 Relaxed environment allows children to talk with staff and one another most of the day.

5.1 Staff frequently ask questions that children are interested in answering.*

5.2 Many staff-child conversations during indoor free play.*

5.3 Staff respond positively to children's communication and encourage them to talk more (Ex: listens with interest to child who is able to speak at length; provides words to help child explain what she wants; responds positively to children's questions and follows through with children's requests).*

5.4 Staff help children communicate verbally with one another (Ex: ask them to "use their words" if fighting over a toy, and follow through appropriately; remind child to say "excuse me" when trying to move past another child; begin topic of conversation and help all children contribute).*
Observe twice

7.1 Staff ask many questions that require longer answers (Ex: questions that begin with "how", "what if", "why", "tell me about").*
Observe twice

7.2 Many staff-child conversations during gross motor free play and routines.*

7.3 Staff-child conversations go beyond classroom activities and materials (Ex: include social talk about home and family life; activities in the community; feelings; other non-school topics).*
Observe once

Notes for Clarification

*A score of *NA* is not allowed for this Item. If, during the observation, no books are used with the children, score all 1s *Yes* and the remaining indicators *No*. The books do not have to be read from beginning to end, but the time should allow a meaningful experience.

In scoring, consider only the staff who are usually in the classroom working with the children. For the definition of "staff", see Explanation of Terms Used Throughout the Scale.

Electronic books are considered in this Item as long as they are not animated, (no moving pictures or print). Animated e-books are considered in Item 27.

Appropriate use of technology.

1.1, 1.3, 3.1, 5.1, 7.3. "Use books" can include reading to children, pointing out pictures in a book, informally telling the story shown in pictures, listening to the child tell the story, talking about the book's contents, and other activities in which the staff and children share books together. "Reading books" means that the staff actually read the print content of the book to the children.

1.4, 7.1. "Inappropriate" means that the book is not age- and developmentally appropriate for the children in the group. In addition, a book might cause a child to be frightened, such as a book that contains graphic violence or frightening content. Inappropriate books may give a negative social message, showing stereotypes of a group of people, prejudice, or give the message that it is good to use aggression to solve social issues. This would be true in many fairy tales, for example where the good character kills the "bad" character, instead of working out problems without harming one another.

5.2. Score *Yes* if all children are engaged and no additional support is needed.

5.4. This Indicator requires that staff draw attention to books several times during the observation. Do not give credit for staff telling children to use books as a time-filler during transitions, especially if it is observed that children show little interest in the books at that time.

7.3. Do not count staff reading to a few children during a time when all children are required to be looking at books as a whole group.

7.4. This use of books with the children can be observed as a teacher reminds children of using books to discover information about something that came up in the past, or during the observation as a teacher refers children to a book to find information. It can be staff-initiated or can happen when a child shows curiosity or a need for an answer, and staff lead them to a book and help them use it.

Inadequate		Minimal		Good		Excellent
1	2	3	4	5	6	7

14. Staff use of books with children*

1.1 Staff do not use books with children during the observation.*

1.2 Book times are unpleasant or not engaging for many of the children (Ex: children forced to listen; punitive atmosphere; children can't see book; children's reactions are treated as interruptions).

1.3 Staff reading or use of books with children is dull, disinterested, and/or unenthusiastic.*

1.4 Inappropriate book observed being used with the children (Ex: reading a book that has frightening content, gives a negative social message, or shows prejudice; that is too long or too difficult to understand).*

3.1 Staff read a book with children at least once during the observation.*

3.2 Book time is arranged to encourage children's engagement (Ex: children can easily see the book; crowding does not cause problems; books used that interest children; appropriate length).

3.3 The majority of children appear to be engaged for most of the time when books are used (Ex: children may lose interest for short period, but then become interested again; one child is not interested but others are).

3.4 Staff show some interest and enjoyment in books.

5.1 Staff read books to children during the observation, either to the whole group, to a small group, or individually.*

5.2 Accommodations are made for children who require additional support during book time (Ex: children not fluent in classroom language, with developmental delays, or who do not do well in large groups have special provision, such as smaller group).*

5.3 All children participating in the activity are actively engaged during each book time (Ex: staff is supportive and reads with interest; children appear to enjoy book time and pay attention).

5.4 Staff show much interest and enjoyment in books (Ex: read with animation; responds to children who are looking at books).*

7.1 Appropriate books that relate to current classroom activities or themes are read to or used with children.*
Observe once

7.2 Staff and children discuss the content of a book in a way that engages children.
Observe once

7.3 Staff use books informally with children, with more than one example observed.*
Observe twice

7.4 Staff use books with children to help answer questions and to provide information on things that children are curious about.*
Observe once

Notes for Clarification

*An inspection of each and every book is not necessary to complete this Item. When there are large numbers of books accessible (more than 35), select a random sample of those the children are most likely to access. For example, do not closely inspect books that are packed tightly onto shelves or at the bottom of baskets or crates. Do not give credit for books that are incomplete, badly torn, or otherwise in poor repair. Books are considered appropriate when the level of content is right for the ages and interests of the children. Inappropriate books may contain topics and illustrations that are frightening, show violence, or give negative social messages, such as a biased point of view or using aggression to solve problems.

1.1, 3.1. Score 1.1 *Yes* if books are accessible for less than 25 minutes of the observation in a program of any length. The 25-minute requirement in 3.1 is required during the observation for a program of any length.

5.1. "Many" means at least 20 books for 10 children, or 30 books for 15 children, plus one more for each additional child. Calculate based on the highest number of children attending at any time.

5.3. The reading interest center must meet the requirements of "interest center" found in the Explanation of Terms Used Throughout the Scale. A rug is acceptable as a comfortable furnishing if accompanied by some other softness, such as pillows, a large soft toy that children can lean on, or a child-sized bean bag. Some harder furnishings, such as a cushioned chair with wooden arms or a child's wooden rocking chair, would also count here.

5.4. Do not consider children's use of books when children are required to each look at a book as a large group.

7.1. To determine whether a wide selection is accessible, each book does not have to be inspected in detail. It is not required that observers go through books to see if certain topics are represented within a book. Rather, look at the general topics covered (usually by looking at a sample of the covers) to find out whether there is significant variety among the books. For example, look for books about people, feelings, nature/science, math, cultures, varying race, males and females, jobs/work, health or self-help skills, sports/hobbies, abilities. *All topics do not need to be present, and other topics might be included to create the variety.*

7.2. "Current classroom activities" requires that subjects being discussed due to special interests in the classroom change, either due to curriculum plans, children's interests, or times of the year. If the books are not obvious in the environment, do not carry out an extensive search to find them.

15. Encouraging children's use of books*

1.1 Less than 10 intact books accessible.*

1.2 Children frequently told to use books as a time-filler during transitions, and most children are not interested.

1.3 Most accessible books are not appropriate (Ex: meant for younger or older children; have inappropriate content; frightening; give a negative social message; in very poor repair).

1.4 No obvious place to use books (Ex: books are scattered throughout the classroom, even in areas of active play where reading would be difficult).

3.1 At least 15 books are accessible to children for at least 25 minutes during the observation.*

3.2 Accessible books include some fantasy and some factual.

3.3 Most accessible books appear to be in good repair and generally appropriate for children.

3.4 Some books gathered together and stored for easy access so that children can reach them and have a place to use them (Ex: not crammed into a tightly packed shelf; not too high).

5.1 Many books accessible for at least 1 hour during the observation.*

5.2 Children show interest in accessible books (Ex: child chooses to use books in the cozy area during free play; looks at book in science center).
Observe once

5.3 Books are organized in a defined reading interest center, with a place to store the books for easy access and a space with comfortable furnishing to use them.*

5.4 Staff show positive interest when children choose to use books independently.*

7.1 A wide selection of books is accessible.*

7.2 At least 5 books that relate to current classroom activities or themes are accessible and easily observed.*

7.3 Most accessible books are displayed in order to encourage book use (Ex: books not crowded on shelf; many covers easily seen).

43

Notes for Clarification

*All print considered when scoring this Item must be easy for children to see clearly.

3.1. To be considered as meeting the requirements of this Indicator, the print must be obviously connected to what is pictured. At least one-third of visible print in the display materials must meet this requirement. For example, picture/word labels on shelves; pictures of children showing varied emotions, with the words next to each; letters of the alphabet with pictures of words that begin with that letter.

3.2. To give credit, children must both be able to clearly see the print being read and hear the words or sounds. This can happen as staff write words while a child watches, such as when writing a child's name and talking about the letters and the sounds they represent.

3.3. It is not necessary to ensure that exactly all children's printed names are used in the classroom, but it should appear that this is a usual practice.

5.1. Do not consider materials displayed for adults, such as activity plans, schedules, menus, fire drill procedures, etc.

5.3. Evidence of this requirement might be found in display materials, such as charts or children's artwork with their comments written on it, or staff are observed writing for the children. Consider work in the display materials only if it is obvious that it has been posted recently.

7.1. "Current classroom topics" requires that the special-interest subjects being discussed in the classroom change periodically, either due to curriculum plans, children's interests, or times of the year. If the materials are not obvious in the environment, do not carry out an extensive search to find them.

7.2. This must be observed. Displayed evidence does not count for this Indicator. Give credit if observed twice.

7.4. Observe evidence in the display material being used. For example, staff points out the steps in a procedure or children discuss picture-word instructions.

16. Becoming familiar with print*

1.1 Print only used in a way that is not clearly associated with spoken language or pictures (Ex: word labels used without pictures; rote word or letter identification expected with no clues as to meaning).

1.2 Staff respond negatively when children show little or no interest in activities used to teach letters or words (Ex: scold child or send to time-out; make child work on letter activity until finished even though others get to play).

1.3 No connection is made between print in the classroom and its immediate function for children (Ex: word labels on furniture not used in a meaningful way; children's printed names not used to show possessions)

1.4 Children who are not yet able are often asked to identify or write letters or words (Ex: children lose interest in group during letter naming activity; struggle over writing names).
Observe twice

3.1 Some visible print is combined with pictures so that children can understand meanings or sounds that go with what they are viewing.*

3.2 Staff point out and read print to children (Ex: read names on displayed pictures; point to words in books; sing alphabet song while pointing to letters).*
Observe once

3.3 Printed names of children used in the classroom (Ex: on cubbies, put on artwork; name cards used by children to show they are present; more advanced child encouraged to write own name).*

5.1 Most visible print is combined with pictures.*

5.2 Staff show that print is a useful tool as they explain how or why they use it (Ex: label child's toy, or encourage more able child to do it to be sure that it is taken home; write note with child to remind parent to bring in snack; child asks what is for lunch and staff points to and reads menu for the day).

5.3 Staff write down what a child says, more advanced child encouraged to write (Ex: staff write what child says about artwork; makes chart based on child input during small-group time; more advanced and interested child writes in book he creates).*
Observe once.

7.1 Picture/print materials relate to current classroom topics and show a variety of words.*

7.2 Staff observed writing down what a child says in a way that engages the child.*
Observe twice

7.3 Staff frequently point out letters and words as they read print, helping children hear the sounds of the letters or words in a way that engages children.

7.4 Picture/word instructions are used to guide children through multi-step activities (Ex: cooking recipes; planting seeds instruction; proper handwashing).*
Observe once

3.1, 5.2. To give credit, the required numbers of materials should be observed to be accessible during the time required. Do not count duplicates of the same material.

3.2. Score *Yes* if children do this on their own with no staff help.

5.1. There are 4 kinds of fine motor materials required here: **interlocking building materials** (e.g., interlocking blocks of varied sizes, even those that are very large, interlocking logs), **art materials** (e.g., crayons and scissors), **manipulatives** (e.g., stringing beads, pegs and pegboards, sewing cards, table blocks), and **puzzles** (e.g., floor puzzles, framed puzzles). At least 1 of each type must be accessible. Count only materials that are appropriate for the children's age and ability. Do not count materials that are not complete or not functional.

LEARNING ACTIVITIES

17. Fine motor

1.1 Less than 5 different developmentally appropriate fine motor materials accessible during the observation.

1.2 Staff show no interest when children use fine motor materials.

1.3 Fine motor materials generally in poor repair, or incomplete.

3.1 At least 10 different choices of complete, functional, and appropriate fine motor materials accessible for at least 25 minutes during the observation.*

3.2 Staff help solve problems with sharing the materials and have children clean up properly.*

3.3 There is a convenient, comfortable place for children to use the materials (Ex: materials are well-organized for independent use; different types of materials in different bins; table in the activity center; rug area where materials are stored)

3.4 Materials at different levels of difficulty are accessible (Ex: simple and complex puzzles; larger and smaller interlocking blocks; smaller and larger stringing beads).

5.1 Accessible materials include interlocking building materials, manipulatives, puzzles, and art materials that encourage fine motor skills, such as pencils for scribbling, drawing, or writing, or scissors for cutting.*

5.2 Materials required in 5.1 are accessible for at least 1 hour during the observation.*

5.3 Staff show some interest as children use fine motor materials (Ex: ask short answer questions about color or shape; participate in play).

7.1 Staff show more extended interest in what children create/do with the materials (Ex: have conversations with children about what they make; show how to use materials; have children select materials of appropriate interest and difficulty). *Observe for 2 different children*

7.2 Containers and/or accessible storage shelves have labels to encourage self-help.

7.3 Staff use their comments and questions to help children expand their use of exact words, understand relevant concepts, or associate spoken language with written language (Ex: watch and talk about what makes the gears move or how the blocks interlock; discuss the picture the puzzle pieces made; print what the child said on his drawing or on a photo of her construction). *Observe once*

Notes for Clarification

*Categories of art materials are (1) **drawing materials,** such as crayons, nontoxic watercolor markers, pencils, chalk;(2) **paints,** such as tempera, watercolor sets, finger paint; (3) **materials to create three-dimensional objects,** such as play dough, wood scraps, clay, boxes; (4) **collage materials,** such as cloth scraps, yarn, colorful or textured paper scraps;(5) **tools,** such as scissors, tape, hole punches, rulers, stencils, stamps with pads. All materials must be accompanied by paper, as needed, or another surface for use when carrying out artwork.

1.1 "Rarely accessible" means activities with art materials are not offered during the observation, or all children do not have the opportunity to participate if they wish, or the time offered is too short to be satisfying to the children.

1.1, 3.1, 5.1. When drawing materials are observed being used for coloring predesigned pages, such as coloring books or worksheets, count use of the materials in Item 17. Fine motor, but not in this Item.

1.2, 3.2, 5.2, 7.1, 7.2. Look for evidence in what is observed as children use art materials and also in the display materials.

5.1. To give credit, the required numbers of materials should be observed to be accessible during the whole hour.

5.2. In scoring, consider how children use art materials during the observation and children's art displayed in the room. Also look at lesson or activity plans if there is evidence that they are followed. There should be evidence of no more than two examples of teacher-directed projects where children follow an example.

5.3. "Conversations" require a back-and-forth exchange between two people. Do not give credit if staff use only short-answer questions, give instructions, or manage behavior.

7.2. This Indicator refers to the theme or topic of interest currently being discussed on the day of the observation, not to a theme that was discussed in the past.

7.3. Captions can be observed in obviously recently displayed artwork.

18. Art*

1.1 Art materials are rarely accessible to the children.*

1.2 No individual expression encouraged when children use art materials (Ex: coloring worksheets; whole group produces same project where work of all children looks similar; children must follow an example).*

1.3 No staff involvement or staff involvement only to ensure that children follow example exactly and complete project, prevent messes or misuse of materials.

3.1 At least 1 drawing material accessible for 25 minutes during the observation (Ex: sufficient number of crayons or markers in usable condition, with paper or other suitable drawing surface).*

3.2 Some individual expression with art materials is observed as children use art materials, or observed in the display (Ex: children allowed to do free drawing; paints at easel for children to use in own way; play dough used without cookie cutters).*

3.3 Some positive staff involvement with children using art materials (Ex: staff make comments to show appreciation about a child's work; identify colors or shapes seen in a child's creation).
Observe once

5.1 At least 1 material from each category is accessible for 1 hour during the observation.*

5.2 Most art activities allow children to use materials in their own way.*

5.3 Staff have conversations with interested children about their work (Ex: "Tell me about your picture." "How did you make that clay form?").*
Observe twice

7.1 Staff observed to teach children to use more complex art materials appropriately or all children are able to use them appropriately (Ex: demonstrate use of watercolor paints; create 3-D constructions with cardboard boxes or wood scraps; simple paper folding or cutting).*

7.2 Some art activities are related to current classroom themes or interests (Ex: drawings of a trip to the zoo; paintings of fall colors; collage based on a recently read favorite book).*

7.3 Staff write captions dictated by interested children about their artwork or help older children to write captions for themselves if they wish to (Ex: "You said, 'This is my new puppy.' See, I wrote your words. Your mommy can read it to you later too!")*

Notes for Clarification

*This Item is to be scored based upon the daily music experiences children are observed to have, including access to musical instruments, recorded music, singing, or movement activities. Do not count experiences provided by a special music teacher who is not present daily or almost daily, even if the music teacher is present during the observation.

3.1. If recorded music is played by staff, this counts as one material that is accessible to the children. Each complete musical instrument counts as one material.

3.2. Score *Yes* if no background music is used. To score *Yes*, staff should not be observed reading to the group of children or singing with them while unrelated music is on; the music should not be so loud that it can be heard across the whole classroom, or interfere so that voices must be raised in order to talk, or interrupt quiet activities.

3.4. "Generally" means at least 75% of the children. If no teacher-led group music activity is observed, score *NA*.

5.1. "Many music materials" means that there are at least 10 instruments in good condition accessible to the children, or if used at group time there must be at least 1 instrument for each child participating. Credit cannot be given if all materials are of the same type. A player of recorded music can be given credit as 1 music material, whether played by staff or children during the observation.

5.4. If no music is observed, score *No*. If all children readily participate, score *Yes*. Positive encouragement is acceptable, but forcing uninterested children to participate is not (for example, pulling children to their feet to make them dance; reprimanding a child for not singing along).

7.1. Score *NA* if no group music is observed. If children are required to participate in group music, but become engaged with interest and no problems occur, then credit can be given for this Indicator. Score *No* if children continue to show a lack of participation or interest and they are not allowed to participate in other activities that are more interesting to them.

7.3. *NA* is permitted only if all of the children in the group are under the age of 4.

Inadequate		Minimal		Good		Excellent
1	2	3	4	5	6	7

19. Music and movement*

1.1 No music and/or movement experiences for children. (Ex: no music materials accessible; no singing; no recorded music used).

1.2 Loud background music is on for most of the observation, and interferes with ongoing activities (Ex: staff or children must raise voices to be heard above music; stays on during quiet circle times; raises noise level in noisy room).

3.1 At least 3 music materials accessible to the children for at least 25 minutes during the observation (Ex: simple music instruments; music toys; recorded music player with recorded music; radio on with appropriate music).*

3.2 Background music does not interfere with any other activity.*

3.3 Staff engaged in singing with children during the observation, either formally or informally.

3.4 Staff-led group music activities are pleasant and children generally appear to be engaged.*
NA permitted

5.1 Many music materials accessible for 1 hour during free play.*

5.2 During free play, staff observed singing or doing dance/movement activity with the children.

5.3 Some movement/dance activity observed.

5.4 Staff positively encourage children to participate (Ex: dance; clap, or sing along).*

7.1 Children not required to participate in group music if not interested; interesting alternate activities accessible.*
NA permitted

7.2 Staff point out rhyming words in songs, identify sound repetition such as consonants or vowels, or do finger plays where children use gestures or actions to act out meaning of words.
Observe once

7.3 Staff encourage older preschoolers to experiment with rhyming in songs, thinking of new words that rhyme (Ex: model the practice and then help children to think of another word).*
Observe once
NA permitted

51

Notes for Clarification

1.1, 3.1, 5.1, 7.1. Although there are many types of play materials that are used in construction play, there are 2 types of blocks that are considered in these Indicators—**unit blocks** and **large hollow blocks.** This item does not consider interlocking block materials of any type or size, nor does it consider smaller blocks (where most have sides of less than 2 inches), such as table blocks, alphabet blocks, or inch cubes. Unit blocks are usually made of wood, plastic, or hard foam. Within a set, you will find varied shapes, all of which relate in scale. For example, four small square blocks, each measuring 1 unit, will be equal in size to one longer rectangular block of 4 units. Large hollow blocks allow children to build larger structures, and can be made of wood, cardboard, or plastic. They can be found in same-size sets or in sets of varied sizes or shapes. They are larger than unit blocks.

3.1, 5.1. "Accessories" are toys to be used with blocks in block play. Accessories should *enhance*, rather than detract from block play. They must be stored with the blocks in a way that gives children the message that they are to be used as part of block play. Types of accessories required for this item include (1) **small people,** (2) **vehicles,** (3) **animals,** (4) other accessories used to enhance block play, such as road signs, fences, trees, small buildings, etc. If use of vehicles or other toys interferes with building, do not count the toys as accessories.

3.1, 5.1. To determine how many blocks are needed, consider the developmental abilities of the children in the group being observed. Younger preschoolers will need fewer blocks than older preschoolers who are able to build more extensive structures—tall and complex buildings or wide, far-reaching road systems.

3.2. The amount of *space* needed for the structures will differ based on the age group, with younger preschoolers generally needing a smaller block space than older preschool children, who need much larger areas to accommodate their constructions. Space used for block play must not be used for other purposes that interfere with the use of blocks. Also consider the size of the blocks that are accessible to be used in the space.

3.3. For blocks to be "organized by type," different sets of blocks (e.g., wooden unit, plastic unit, cardboard large hollow, home-made) should not be jumbled together. However, it is not required that the block shapes or sizes are separated in storage.

5.2. To give credit, the system must be observed to work for the children. Blocks must be organized by shape/size and type, with labels on the shelves that show images or outlines of the blocks to be stored there. The use of printed words only on labels is not given credit. If accessories are stored in bins, both shelves and containers must have labels. Very few, if any, exceptions should be observed.

5.3. If other materials are included in the block center (such as fine motor interlocking construction materials, carpentry tools, floor puzzles, books on construction), and use of these materials interferes with block play in any way, then credit cannot be given for a special block interest center. However, if the interest center is very large and there is enough space for the required 3 children to build sizable independent structures with the blocks at the same time, then credit can be given.

5.4. In some cases, more than one block area may be used during the observation. For example, there might be a block interest center in the classroom and another in the gym. The time these two centers are used can be combined to calculate total time accessible. To be considered in calculating accessibility for 1 hour's time, all block centers included in the time calculation must meet requirements in 5.1–5.3.

7.2. Evidence in current display materials can be considered when scoring.

20. Blocks

1.1 No blocks accessible for children's use.*

1.2 Staff show little or no interest in children's block play (Ex: do not encourage block-building; interact only to stop quarrels or insist that children clean up after block play; do not talk about their play or show appreciation for their constructions).

3.1 Enough blocks and accessories accessible for at least 2 children to build sizeable independent structures at the same time, for at least 25 minutes during the observation.*

3.2 Enough clear floor space for 2 children to build sizeable independent structures.*

3.3 Blocks and accessories are organized by type.*

3.4 Some positive involvement by staff when children use blocks (Ex: make positive comments about what children are building; show some interest in children's work with blocks; ask children to identify shapes).

5.1 Enough space, unit blocks, and accessories from 3 categories accessible for 3 children to build sizeable independent structures at the same time.*

5.2 Almost all blocks and accessories are stored on open, labeled shelves (Ex: labeled with pictures or outline of blocks).*

5.3 Special block interest center set aside, with storage and suitable building surface (Ex: flat rug or other steady surface; area out of traffic).*

5.4 Block interest center accessible for play for at least 1 hour during the observation.*

5.5 Staff have many conversations with interested children about their block play (Ex: ask questions about what children are building or their favorite shapes to use; talk about pictures of structures with the children).

7.1 Large hollow blocks are accessible for use in a suitably large area where play can be very active.*

7.2 Staff link written language to children's block play (Ex: write children's comments about what they have built; take photos and write captions; write about shapes children used in structures).*

7.3 Staff point out the math concepts that are demonstrated in unit blocks in a way that interests children (Ex: discuss "more" and "less", relationships in size or shape: "Look, these two squares make a rectangle, just like this one."; number of blocks; measurement).

Observe once

Notes for Clarification

*Dramatic play is pretending or making believe. This type of play occurs when children act out roles. Even though children often pretend with small toy people, toy animals, vehicles, or other small pretend-play toys such as doll houses, such small pretend-play materials often found in the block or fine motor areas do not count in scoring this Item. Activities used to teach children to follow specific sequences to properly complete household chores, such as table washing or silver polishing activities, are also not counted to meet the requirements of this Item. Children must be free to use the materials in their own way, as part of their own make-believe play, to get credit for this Item.

3.1. The materials must be accessible for at least 25 minutes during the 3-hour observation, prorated for shorter programs.

5.1. This Indicator requires that there are many and varied materials. It also requires that within the many and varied materials, basic materials like dolls and play foods are present. However, just providing the specified materials does not meet the requirement of many and varied. Children should have additional props to use, either additional housekeeping toys or materials from other themes, such as **different kinds of work** (e.g., recognizable equipment and clothing identified with office staff, doctors, shopkeepers, restaurant staff, firefighters, police); **fantasy** (e.g., a variety of non-frightening "make believe" costumes and props); and **leisure** (e.g., camping, sports). To give credit, there should be a wealth of materials for children to use in their pretend play.

5.2. See the definition of "interest center" in the Explanation of Terms Used Throughout the Scale.

7.2. Look for recent evidence of such activity, either in the display, in props that have obviously been added to allow acting out of current topics, or in what is talked about in the classroom.

21. Dramatic play*

1.1 Not enough materials, furniture for dramatic play for 2 children to be happily engaged (Ex: children compete for toys; dramatic play materials in poor repair; play encroaches on other areas).

1.2 Most dramatic play materials are broken, incomplete, or hard to access (Ex: few dishes and little play food; sink missing in kitchen cabinet; dress-up clothes stuffed into small drawer that is hard to open).

1.3 Staff usually ignore children in the dramatic play area, except to stop disruptive behavior (Ex: staff settle conflicts, manage rotation of turns, or ask children to lower their voices).

3.1 Some dramatic play materials and furniture accessible for at least 25 minutes during the observation so children can act out family roles themselves (Ex: dress-up clothes; housekeeping props; dolls).*

3.2 Staff are somewhat responsive to the children during dramatic play (Ex: helps in putting on some of the dramatic play clothes, or to dress a doll).

3.3 Most of the staff interaction is positive or neutral (Ex: talk while joining in play; ask about what children are doing; comment on the play).

5.1 Many and varied dramatic play materials, enough for number of children allowed, are accessible, including dolls, child-sized furniture, play foods and cooking/eating utensils, dress-up clothes for boys and girls.*

5.2 A dramatic play interest center meeting requirements in 5.1 is accessible for at least 1 hour during the observation (Ex: most storage is reasonably organized; the materials are easy to access).*

5.3 Staff carry on conversations with the children as they play, joining in but not taking over (Ex: relate children's play to their home experiences; discuss the roles children are playing; encourage play based on field trip).
Observe twice

7.1 At least 4 clear examples to represent diversity are included for dramatic play (Ex: dolls of different races/cultures; foods of different cultures; equipment used by people with disabilities).

7.2 Staff talk with children about print and numbers in dramatic play in a way that is meaningful to the children (Ex: discuss menus with prices for restaurants; help children make signs and price tags for store play; pretend to phone people using a home-made telephone book).*
Observe once

Notes for Clarification

1.1, 3.1, 5.1. "Nature/science materials" include (1) **living things** the children can observe closely or care for (house plants, pets, an outside garden); (2) **natural objects** (bird's nest; leaves; insects in transparent plastic; rocks; seashells; collection of seeds); (3) **factual books/nature-science picture games**; (4) **tools** (magnifying glasses; magnets); and (5) **sand or water with toys** (measuring cups; digging tools and containers). In searching for nature/science materials, they must be easily found to give credit. One should not have to search through large numbers of books to find any nature/science books, dig through stacks of puzzles all on top of one another, or look for plants up high in a corner that the children rarely pay attention to.

3.3, 5.1. Sand or water, with appropriate toys, can be located indoors or outdoors. Toys to use with sand or water must always be provided. When sand and water are accessible at different times, each can be considered when determining if an Indicator's time requirement is met. For example, times for sand outdoors and water indoors can each be considered and added together to meet the 1-hour requirement in 5.1.

5.1. The area must include at least 5 nature/science books. All 15 required materials must be accessible for the full-time requirement. Be sure that the area meets the requirements of the definition found in the Terms Used Throughout the Scale. Provisions for sand/water are not required to be located within the interest center, but each can be counted as 1 of the 15 materials if accessible during the observation for the amount of time required.

7.1. Some obvious current evidence must be present to score *Yes*, either occurring during the observation or found in obviously recent display materials. For example, a teacher is observed setting up an activity and showing children how to do it, or children independently carry out the activities. At least 2 different sources of evidence must be observed to score *Yes*. Examples might include sorting leaves or shells by shape, color, or size; measuring rain and keeping a chart to show continuing findings; taking photos of clouds and comparing the different types; using magnets to sort materials into groups of those attracted and those not attracted.

22. Nature/science

1.1 No nature/science materials accessible.*

1.2 Staff do not talk about nature/science with the children during the observation (Ex: mention weather, seasons; read factual book on animals; mention temperature of water).

1.3 Staff show a lack of interest, or dislike, for the natural world (Ex: show fear of a large spider instead of cautious respect; ignore natural occurrences).

3.1 At least 5 developmentally appropriate nature/science materials from at least 2 categories are accessible for at least 25 minutes during the observation.*

3.2 Staff talk about nature/science with the children during the observation (Ex: do weather chart; ask names of animals in pictures; talk about healthful food at snack).
Observe once

3.3 Sand or water, with appropriate toys, is accessible for at least 25 minutes during the observation.*

5.1 At least 15 nature/science materials, some from each of the 5 listed categories, are accessible in a clearly defined nature science interest center, for at least 1 hour during the observation.*

5.2 Staff use and talk about nature/science materials with the children.
Observe once

5.3 Staff model concern for the environment (Ex: remind children to turn off water or turn off light to save resources; recycle; discuss how insects can be helpful).
Observe once

7.1 Staff initiate activities for measuring, comparing, or sorting using nature/science materials (Ex: show children how to sort seashells by color, shape, or size; arrange pinecones from biggest to smallest; chart rainfall for a month to discuss dry and wet times; predict weights of various natural objects).*

7.2 One or more pets/plants present that children can easily observe, help care for, and that are talked about with the children (Ex: classroom fish tank, hamster, gerbil; birds that are seen visiting filled bird feeder).
Observe once

Notes for Clarification

*Note that there are 3 math Items. Become familiar with each before scoring.

For this item, **"math materials"** are those that children can play with to learn and practice math concepts. Posters/books and other displayed materials are not counted here, nor are play materials such as toy telephones or cash registers that have numbers printed on them; consider such materials in Item 25, Understanding written numbers. All materials considered must be appropriate, meaning that the materials are safe, have no negative social messages, challenge and interest children while not leading to constantly wrong answers or frustration. *Although some math materials might fit into more than 1 category, do not assign any material to more than 1 category.*

Types of math materials to observe for this Item include:

1) **counting/comparing quantities,** such as unifix cubes with number trays; small objects to count into numbered containers; games that require children to figure out more or less; chart and graph activities for children to use by placing materials into cells; dominoes; playing cards; games with dice; abacus; pegboards with numbers printed and holes to match; puzzles where written numbers are matched to quantities on a puzzle piece; beads with bead patterns

2) **measuring/comparing sizes and parts of wholes (fractions),** such as measuring cups and spoons with material to measure; balance scale with things to weigh; rulers, yardsticks, tape measures with things to measure; thermometers; foot size measurer; height chart if regularly used to measure children's growth; games with parts to divide and put back together to make the whole (fractions); puzzles with geometric shapes that must be put together; games where halves are matched to the whole (fractions); shapes-matching games where geometric shapes are divided into parts (fractions)

3) **familiarity with shapes,** such as shape sorters; puzzles with different geometric shapes; unit blocks with image/outline labels on shelves used during clean up; geoboards (boards with pegs to which rubber bands are attached to make shapes); attribute blocks of different sizes, shapes, colors; parquetry blocks with patterns; magnetic shapes; shape stencils

1.3, 3.3, 5.4, 7.1, 7.2, 7.3. Math **"activities"** are teacher-initiated and -directed and go beyond children's use of materials in free play with teacher input. Generally the staff would have to set up specific materials to be used, with an intended purpose of math learning. They may be offered during free play with children choosing to participate, or they may be carried out during small-group or whole-group times. Appropriate math activities must be used with all children at some point, but not necessarily each child every day. Look to be sure math is not used only with more advanced children. Less advanced children are able to compare numbers to determine smaller or larger; very advanced children begin to use addition and subtraction. Less advanced children begin to tell one shape from another; more advanced discuss rotation of shapes and the addition of shapes to make new shapes.

3.3. For these activities, children can be in large groups, small groups, or working individually. Consider all math activities when scoring.

5.3. If it is not observed that a child uses fingers to represent a number, or the staff do not actively encourage this, score *No*. For example, if the staff use a number of fingers to show a number, but do not encourage the children do so, then credit would not be given.

7.1. Do not count evidence in the display materials unless they are used for math during the observation.

Inadequate		Minimal		Good		Excellent
1	2	3	4	5	6	7

23. Math materials and activities*

1.1 Few or no appropriate math materials in the room for children to use in play.

1.2 Staff are never observed to show children how to use math materials, or participate when materials are used in play.

1.3 Most math activities do not keep most children engaged (Ex: not appropriate for developmental level; children frequently lose attention or are frustrated with activities; children rarely select math activities independently).*

3.1 At least 2 different, appropriate math materials from each of the 3 categories (counting/comparing quantities; measuring/comparing sizes/fractions; familiarity with shapes) are accessible for at least 25 minutes during the observation.

3.2 Staff sometimes give information or ask basic questions about math as children play with the materials (Ex: name puzzle shapes; count number of beads in a pattern; talk about "big" and "little"; ask "how many?" or "what shape?").
Observe once

3.3 Math activities used engage most of the participating children (Ex: most children are interested in calendar activities that are math related; enjoy rote counting at group time).*

5.1 At least 10 different appropriate math materials, with at least 3 from each of the 3 categories listed, are accessible for at least 1 hour during the observation.

5.2 Staff frequently join in children's play with math materials (Ex: ask questions; respond to children's questions, show enthusiasm; teach children to use materials.
Observe 3 examples

5.3 Staff encourage children to use their fingers to represent numbers (Ex: in songs; to show age; while reading counting book).*

5.4 Staff encourage use of math materials/activities and help children use them successfully (Ex: set up and show how to do balance scale activity; show children how to use shape matching game and help children tell which shapes go together).*

7.1 Staff relate math materials/activities to current topics of interest (Ex: make chart on what children ate for breakfast; insect counting game added when talking about insects; big/small leaf game offered when talking about autumn).*
Observe once

7.2 Staff ask children questions about math materials/activities that stimulate reasoning (Ex: "What do you think would happen if we put all the feathers on one side of the scale and a block on the other side?" "What will happen to the square shape if we add another square next to it?").*
Observe once

7.3 Some appropriate math activities requiring more teacher input are used (Ex: sort seashells by type on a chart and compare more and less; read thermometer to chart daily temperature; measure while doing cooking activity).*
Observe once

Notes for Clarification

*"Daily events" consist of the parts of the daily schedule, such as play times, non-math large and small group times, transitions, and routines. "Math in daily events" is the use of math words and concepts during non-math activities. Such experiences help children see the value and use of math in their daily lives, and help them to generalize math learning to many types of experiences.

1.2. Staff math talk must be obviously negative to score *Yes*. Often there will be a threat implied in the use of the math talk, such as "If you do not settle down by the time I count to 10, then you will not be going outside." Math talk might be used in a positive manner, such as a challenge to see how fast children can clean up, but as long as there is no threat implied, do not consider here.

3.3. This must be observed once to score *Yes*. Score *NA* if no group time is observed.

5.1. Children's use of materials alone (e.g., measuring cups to serve foods) does not count here. To give credit, staff must add math words to encourage understanding

5.2. Both staff and child are required to contribute to the conversation with interest.

24. Math in daily events*

1.1 Staff do not use math words or ideas when talking to children during daily events (Ex: "Five more minutes until clean up." "First we will get our coats, and second, we will go outside." "Please sit at the square table.").

1.2 Staff math talk is observed being used in a threatening or punitive manner with the children once during the observation (Ex: "I'm going to count to three, and if you do not do it, you go to time-out").*

1.3 Staff become irritated or negative with children if they do not understand and respond appropriately to math talk (Ex: Staff member is obviously annoyed when she says, "Take only two banana slices," and child takes three, or when she says "Only three people in this center," and a fourth child enters the center anyway).

3.1 Staff occasionally count or use other math words during transitions or routines (Ex: count while children wash hands; tell amount of time until clean-up; use "first", "second", "third" when giving directions).
Observe once

3.2 Staff sometimes use math talk as children play with non-math materials in non-math areas (Ex: count blocks in a child's tower; match blocks to size and shape labels during clean-up; ask how many pieces of toy pizza fit into the pizza pan; mention numbers of colors used in child's painting while pointing them out).
Observe once

3.3 Staff use math talk referring to daily events during large-group time (Ex: counting who is present and absent; reminding children how many days are left before the weekend).*
*Observe once;
NA permitted if no group time*

5.1 Staff encourage math learning as part of daily routines (Ex: explain setting table; name rectangular and round tables when saying where to put plates and cups; counting to 20 while washing hands; using measuring cup to serve portions at meals).*
Observe twice

5.2 Staff engage children in conversations about math as they play in non-math areas (Ex: discuss using measuring cups to water plant; count how many teacups are needed for dolls; talk about how to measure feet in play shoe store).*
Observe twice

7.1 Staff help children to connect printed numbers or shapes with everyday use in their environment (Ex: count number of days on calendar until fieldtrip; talk about the numbers on the clock and what they mean in terms of going outside to play; talk about shapes of traffic signs while taking walk).
Observe once

7.2 Staff often use questions while interacting with children in non-math areas to encourage children to explain their own math reasoning (Ex: "How do you know if one more person can play here?" "How did you know if you got enough crayons for everyone?").
Observe once

7.3 Children aged 4 and older given more complex math-related tasks (Ex: count number of children in group to figure out how many are not present; count children to figure out number of napkins needed at lunch; use tape measure to see if table will fit in space; use map while talking about field trip, noting number of blocks or miles traveled).
*Observe once;
NA permitted*

Notes for Clarification

1.2, 3.2. Do not count the page numbers in books, but "Counting" books are considered here.

3.3, 5.3. When children use materials that do not depict written numbers, but staff or children write a number related to the use of the materials, credit can be given.

5.3, 7.3. If children obviously know how to use the materials, staff do not need to teach children how to use them, but must be observed talking about the meaning of the number symbols.

25. Understanding written numbers

1.1 No print numbers in display materials are accompanied by pictures that show what the number means.

1.2 No obvious print numbers found in classroom toys or materials accessible to children.*

1.3 Inappropriate expectations for children to be able to read or write numbers (Ex: reading or writing numbers is too difficult; many mistakes in answering questions; preschoolers required to complete worksheets that are too difficult; staff respond negatively when children are not interested).

3.1 Some print numbers in display materials are accompanied by pictures that show what the number means (Ex: signs for number of children allowed in center accompanied by stick figures to represent the number; poster with numbers and corresponding image showing that number of objects).

3.2 Some play materials with numbers are accessible during the observation (Ex: toy telephones; numbers on play kitchen furnishings; play money; number stencils in writing center).*

3.3 When children play with materials credited in 3.2, staff sometimes point out the numbers and talk about them in a way that interests children.*
Observe once

3.4 Staff sometimes relate print numbers to corresponding number of pictures or objects (Ex: staff member points to number on puzzle or in counting book and helps child count number of pictures that match.).
Observe once

5.1 At least 3 different play materials that help show children the meaning of print numbers are accessible during the observation (Ex: puzzle with number on one piece and that number of dots on matching piece; puzzle with numbered fingers on a hand; matching picture/number card game; simple number card games).

5.2 Materials credited in 5.1 accessible for at least 1 hour during the observation.

5.3 Staff show children how to use materials and talk about the meaning of printed numbers (Ex: count objects with child and read the number; use "first, second, third" as child uses printed number sequence; point out numbers on rulers or thermometers, showing how they indicate differences in size or amount).*
Observe once

7.1 At least 5 different appropriate materials that help children attach meaning to print numbers accessible.

7.2 Materials in 7.1 are accessible for at least 1 hour during the observation.

7.3 Staff frequently show children how to use the number materials and talk about the meaning of printed numbers.*
Observe twice

7.4 Print numbers are sometimes related to number of fingers shown by staff or children (Ex: when reading number book or looking at number poster; when using toys showing numbers).
Observe once

Notes for Clarification

1.1, 3.1, 5.2. Examples of diversity in materials include: dolls of different races or cultures; images in books; easily visible pictures on bulletin boards; music from a variety of cultures played; songs sung in home language of bilingual children enrolled. One example consists of a contrast in diversity. For example, one Asian doll is not an example of diversity, but when accessible near another doll of a different race, the two together become one example of diversity. Examples of diversity may be found in one item, such as a picture with children of two races or a book showing a child with a disability and a child without, or in two separate items, stored close together, such as two books on the shelf, one about people of one race, and another about people of a contrasting race. When considering play foods or dress-up, find contrasting items that each represent a specific culture to create each example. Do not create an example by contrasting one item that is obviously representative of a particular culture with one that is generic. For example, a piece of play pizza (Italian) would need to be contrasted with another play food associated with another culture, such as a taco (Mexican) or sushi (Japanese), not a generic food, such as a common fruit or vegetable. Do not count one item more than once when scoring. Photographs of children in the group are not considered in these Indicators.

1.2, 3.2, 5.2. Categories of diversity for this Item include race, culture, age, ability, and non-traditional or stereotyping gender role.

1.3. Score *Yes* only if there is obvious, deliberate, and repeated prejudice shown. Do not score *Yes* if one isolated example of "politically incorrect" or "culturally insensitive behavior" is observed (e.g., teacher asks children to "sit Indian style."). However, in order to sensitize the staff, any such instance should be mentioned, for example in technical assistance associated with the scale.

3.2, 5.3. If stereotyping or violence is shown with regard to any group, such as some "Cowboy and Indian" toys, then this Indicator should be scored *No*. Gender equity should also be considered here. Portrayals of men/boys doing traditionally male activities and women/girls doing traditionally female activities are acceptable. However, some evidence of non-gender stereotyping must be easily visible to balance the traditional roles shown. Examples of non-stereotyping in gender roles means showing males and females doing similar activities, such as both doing construction, both engaged in sports, or both caring for babies. Do not give credit if gender stereotyping is portrayed negatively in any way. Look for problems that would be easily obvious to the children. It is not necessary to search avidly for negative examples. When historic cultural traditions are represented, the images must be balanced with non-traditional modern representations. For example, if traditional African cultures are represented in materials, then current representations must also be included.

3.3. For example, both boys and girls encouraged to dress up as fire fighters, use hard hats, do carpentry projects, wash dishes in play kitchen, play with dolls.

5.1. Different types of dramatic play materials would include, for example: dolls of different contrasting races; foods or cooking utensils associated with specific cultures; ethnic clothing. Do not consider puppets and block accessories such as small toy people if they are counted for 5.2.

5.2. Do not count dramatic play props considered in 5.1. However, puppets and block accessories such as small toy people can be considered here unless they have been credited in 5.1. When examining books, examples of diversity should be easy to find simply by looking at book covers. If books are difficult for children to access, such as there being too many piled in a basket or tightly packed into shelves, do not consider these easily visible.

7.1. Observed learning activities are required here. Do not consider accessible materials that are a regular part of the environment.

7.2. For example, similarities such as how we all enjoy music or need food, shelter, clothing; how we enjoy different holidays from varied cultures; how foods, songs, or games we enjoy come from different cultures.

Inadequate		Minimal		Good		Excellent
1	2	3	4	5	6	7

26. Promoting acceptance of diversity

1.1 No examples of racial or cultural diversity are easily visible to the children.*

1.2 Materials present only stereotypes of races, cultures, ages, ability, and gender roles.*

1.3 Staff clearly demonstrate prejudice against others (Ex: against child or other adults from different race or cultural group; against person with disability).*

3.1 At least 3 examples of racial/cultural diversity in materials are a regular experience for the children.*

3.2 Materials show diversity in a positive way.*

3.3 Staff usually allow both boys and girls to follow their interests, despite the gender stereotypes associated with some toys and activities.*

5.1 At least 2 different types of dramatic play props representing different races or cultures are included for use in dramatic play.*

5.2 At least 10 easily visible positive examples of diversity, with at least 1 example in each of the following: books, displayed pictures, and accessible play materials.*

5.3 Classroom materials include at least 4 of the 5 types of diversity (race, culture, age, ability, and non-traditional gender role).*

7.1 Inclusion of diversity is observed as part of learning activities, in addition to diversity in materials (Ex: sing songs in more than one language; play music from varying cultures; use sign language for some words).*
Observe once

7.2 Staff have positive conversations with children discussing the benefits of similarities and differences among people.*
Observe once

Notes for Clarification

*If no use of electronic media is observed, score the item *NA* (Not Applicable). Note that e-books or music players are not considered electronic media unless animated with moving pictures or print. Cameras used by the children are not considered here.

Caring for Our Children includes daily and weekly limits for the use of technology. However, these limits are not considered in scoring since they cannot be observed during a 3-hour observation.

1.1, 3.1. To judge whether materials are nonviolent and culturally sensitive, consider the content of the observed materials being used. Unfortunately, many children's videos or TV programs contain violence and are therefore inappropriate, even though they have been created for the children's market. This may include some natural wildlife productions and cartoons. The appropriateness of videos or games brought from children's homes must also be judged, if these materials are used with any child.

1.2, 3.2, 5.2. The intent of these Indicators is to ensure that children participate in play in which they can actively be creative, imaginative, and have hands-on experiences with real materials, rather than spending inordinate amounts of time watching TV or other passive electronic devices. These time limits apply to all programs. Time limits do not apply to children with disabilities using electronic media assistive devices.

3.2. *NA* permitted when no TV/video is used during the observation.

5.2. Score *NA* if only TV or video are used.

5.3. Score *NA* if no electronic media is accessible during free play.

Inadequate		Minimal		Good		Excellent
1	2	3	4	5	6	7

27. Appropriate use of technology*

1.1 Content of observed material used in electronic media is not developmentally appropriate (Ex: violent content; frightening characters or stories; TV program is racially prejudicial; computer game too difficult).*

1.2 Electronic media used with any child for more than 30 minutes.*

1.3 No staff involvement during the observation in use of electronic media beyond starting the equipment.

3.1 All observed materials used are nonviolent, culturally sensitive, and appropriate for the children in the group.*

3.2 Time any child allowed to watch TV/video limited to 10 minutes during the observation.*
NA permitted

3.3 Alternative activities usually accessible most of the time while electronic media are used.

5.1 Observed materials encourage problem-solving rather than rote or random response from children (Ex: encourage matching, sequencing, making thoughtful decisions).

5.2 Other electronic media use limited to 15 minutes per child during the observation (Ex: Smart Board, computer, hand-held games, tablets).*
NA permitted

5.3 Electronic media available as one of many free play activities.*
NA permitted

5.4 Staff are actively involved with children in use of electronic media (Ex: do activity suggested in educational TV program; help child learn to use computer program).
Observe once

7.1 Observed electronic media encourages creativity or vigorous movement (Ex: creative drawing/ painting program on tablet; participate in dance or exercise video).

7.2 Electronic media materials used to support and extend classroom interests, themes, and activities (Ex: staff work together with children to search Internet to find additional material about insects; short video on farms prepares children for field trip).

Notes for Clarification

*When scoring all Indicators, the observer must observe some gross motor activity during the 3-hour observation time. If no gross motor activity is observed, score 1.1, 1.2, and 1.3 *Yes* and all other Indicators *No*. Be sure to consider only the supervision of gross motor activity when scoring. Do not consider more sedentary activities that might be supervised during a gross motor time, such as sand play, reading books, art.

1.3. If very little gross motor activity is observed (less than 10 minutes for all children to participate vigorously), score *Yes*.

5.2. There may be neutral interactions observed with positive, but positive should outweigh neutral, and no negative should be observed to score *Yes*.

5.3. When children are using the gross motor space where more sedentary activities are also provided (such as sand, books, fine motor, or chalk), consider how staff spend their time supervising. To give credit, most staff attention should be supervising gross motor activity.

7.1. "Vigorous gross motor activity" requires that children do enough movement to make them breathe harder and appear to be physically tired.

INTERACTION

28. Supervision of gross motor*

1.1 Little attention paid to children's safety during gross motor time (Ex: children left unattended. even for a short period of time; not enough adults to watch children in space; staff do not pay attention to children even though they are present).

1.2 Most staff-child interaction is negative or unresponsive (Ex: staff seem angry; punitive and over-controlling atmosphere).

1.3 Staff show little or no interest in encouraging children's gross motor development (Ex: don't provide outdoor/indoor strenuous gross motor play even if it is scheduled; give most attention to children doing sedentary activities in gross motor space).*

3.1 Staff pay some attention to children's gross motor activity to ensure children's safety (Ex: do not leave children unattended; attempt to watch all areas of gross motor space; respond to child having trouble).

3.2 Most staff-child interaction is neutral or positive during gross motor time.

3.3 Staff show some interest in children's gross motor activity (Ex: make sure children get scheduled gross motor times; encourage children to run or climb; respond when child calls for attention in gross motor activities).

5.1 Careful supervision occurs in order to ensure children's safety (Ex: remain near the most hazardous equipment when it is being used; locate themselves in a space with a clear view of all areas; stop potentially dangerous activities; actively supervise with attention to all areas and all children).

5.2 Almost all staff-child interaction is positive (Ex: encourage children but do not force participation in exercise; help children work out social issues with a problem-solving approach that satisfies children; stop dangerous activity by explaining the danger and helping children find a safe alternative).*

5.3 Staff show much interest in children who participate in gross motor activity (Ex: do not pay *most* attention to children doing sedentary activities; show enthusiasm when children run, slide, jump; help children learn to use equipment).*

7.1 Staff initiate vigorous gross motor activity for part of the gross motor time (Ex: lead interested children in exercises; organize races for children who want to participate; put on music for dancing).*

7.2 Staff help children develop new skills, including showing how to use equipment that requires more advanced skill (Ex: discuss strategies for pumping on swing; assist children in accomplishing physical goals, such as jumping further, running faster, or kicking ball).

Notes for Clarification

*See definition of "individualized teaching" in Explanation of Terms Used Throughout the Scale.

1.1. "One-size-fits-all" means that staff teach children using the same methods and content for all children, with no attention paid to individual needs related to age, ability, interests, or learning style.

1.2, 3.2, 5.1. "Open-ended" materials/activities are those in which children can use materials appropriately in their own way, with an outcome that is not predetermined by the staff or by the material itself.

1.4. To determine whether children experience much failure, judge whether children can understand the content of most activities and if asked for a response, can do so correctly. Consider only staff-directed activities when scoring. Score *Yes* if failure occurs for most children during any one staff-directed activity, or occurs repeatedly for a few children through all staff-directed activities.

1.4, 5.3. "Staff-directed" activities are initiated by the staff, and children participate. These activities can occur during free play, when children select whether they wish to participate. They can also take place during individual, large-, or small-group times. A teacher-initiated activity can be simple, such as when the teacher asks someone for help with a puzzle or to dance to music she puts on; or they can be complex, as in completing a science experiment in which lots of teacher input is required.

3.4. "Appropriate" activities/materials are safe for the children, right for the children's ages and abilities, and do not give negative social messages. Children will be interested in using the materials and not show frustration when using them, even though they might be challenged. Note that "most" does not require that all materials are appropriate, and it is expected that there will be a range of materials in any classroom to meet varying needs and interests.

5.2. Look for higher-level teaching interactions, such as the addition of more difficult words, expansion of children's ideas related to play, or asking questions that encourage children to explain reasons and ideas related to their play.

29. Individualized teaching and learning*

1.1 Almost all teaching uses a one-size-fits-all approach (Ex: all children must do the same activity in the same way; expectations are not based on children's individual abilities or interests).*

1.2 Few open-ended activities that children can carry out in their own way.*

1.3 Little individualized attention paid to one child at a time as children participate in play (Ex: all children asked same kinds of questions; many rote answers required; teachers involved in other tasks, not free play; teachers ignore children unless there is a problem).

1.4 Children experience much failure during staff-directed activities (Ex: do not know answers; become disengaged).*

3.1 Some teaching uses an individualized approach (Ex: responds to individual interests during circle or meal times).

3.2 Some open-ended activities are accessible during play times (Ex: children can use blocks, dramatic play, or art materials in their own way).*

3.3 Some individualized teaching while children participate in free play (Ex: sit at table and work with each child who comes to participate; sometimes moves to different areas to talk with children or solve problems).

3.4 Most materials/activities accessible to children are appropriate.*

5.1 Many activities observed are open-ended.*

5.2 Staff sometimes circulate through classroom, adding individualized learning to children's activities (Ex: counts blocks with child who built a tower; shows child how to play sorting game; has conversation with child involved in dramatic play).*

5.3 Most staff directed activities allow children to be successful (Ex: children participate with interest; complete tasks within a reasonable amount of time; are not forced to complete tasks that are too difficult).*

7.1 Most teaching is individualized, with few if any exceptions.*

7.2 Much individualized teaching while children participate in free play (Ex: staff circulate often to various areas of room; children's play is enhanced and not interrupted when teaching occurs).

71

Notes for Clarification

*"Interaction" includes both the verbal and nonverbal communications between adults and children.

1.1. If staff rarely responds to the children, score this indicator *Yes*.

1.2. Unpleasant or negative interactions with children give children the message that they are not good, are incompetent, or are not valued for who they are and what they are able to do. For example, staff use threats, seem irritable, show displeasure when a child is not able to complete a difficult task or sit quietly for long periods. Many unpleasant interactions must occur in order to score *Yes*.

3.1. Positive interactions give children the message that they are good, valuable, competent, and appreciated for who they are and what they are able to do. For example, staff praise child for cleaning up, greet child in a way that makes her feel welcome, laugh with child at something funny in a book being read, or show delight with child's creation. Neutral interactions give no obvious message to children.

5.1. "Frequent positive interaction" allows for neutral interactions as well, but the positive must outweigh the neutral. To give credit, there may be few, if any, mildly negative interactions, but none may cause undue distress in the children, and mildly negative examples cannot occur frequently. Note that interactions must be positive (with some neutral) in all large-group, small-group (self-selected or teacher-directed), and individual examples observed. If one of these groupings is not observed, score based on the other types used.

7.1. "Respectful" means that staff interact with all children in a way that lets them know they are valuable human beings. Often this means that staff treat children with no less politeness and concern than they would give to their own friends. It also means that staff treat children as they themselves would prefer to be treated by others. To score *Yes*, staff must show, throughout the observation, that they accept children for who they are and treat them politely and kindly, showing that each child is important. This must be consistently observed across the children, with only minor lapses, if any.

Inadequate		Minimal		Good		Excellent
1	2	3	4	5	6	7

30. Staff-child interaction*

1.1 Staff are not responsive to or involved with the children (Ex: ignore children; seem distant or cold).*

1.2 Interactions with children are often unpleasant.*

1.3 Physical contact is often negative (Ex: roughly restrain child who is misbehaving; push children physically rather than asking them to move; unwanted hugs or tickling).

1.4 The majority of interactions are with large group, rather than with individual children or small groups.

3.1 Some positive interactions with individual children observed.*

3.2 No negative physical contact is observed.

3.3 Staff seem to enjoy being with the children (Ex: show interest in what children are doing; listen attentively to children's comments and respond appropriately).

5.1 Frequent positive staff-child interaction observed throughout the observation, with no long periods of no interaction (Ex: warm eye contact; smiling; sharing interests).*

5.2 There is usually a relaxed, pleasant atmosphere in the group (Ex: few, if any, tense or rushed times; staff and children seem calm and interested in what they are doing; most time is unstressed, with few if any exceptions).

5.3 Staff generally give children a message of warmth through appropriate physical contact (Ex: holds crying child; holds child's hand and listens attentively; pats child's shoulder with admiration).

7.1 Staff are respectful to children and guide them positively (Ex: deal with discipline problems in a calm and reasonable way; listen until child is finished speaking before answering; thank child for doing task).*

7.2 Staff are supportive and comforting when children are anxious, angry, fearful, or hurt.(Ex: is understanding with child who has a problem with a friend; patiently guides angry child).

7.3 Staff are sensitive to children's nonverbal cues, and respond appropriately (Ex: during circle, recognize when children need physical activity and provide it; recognize signs of boredom and provide something interesting to do).

3.2. This Indicator can be scored *Yes*, even when staff do not use "best" positive practices to stop problems. For example, staff might take away a toy a two children are fighting over; say, "Because I said so."; or yell "Walk away!" from across the playground without follow-up. Score *No* if staff ever use harsh discipline, such as yelling angrily or grabbing and yanking a child. It is likely that some minor issues that do not cause undue distress in children may be observed, which staff miss so they are not quickly stopped. At this minimal level, it is acceptable to give these minor problems little weight in scoring. However, if there are many different instances of minor problems, or any problems that cause undue distress (child crying, hurt physically, problem lasts a long time), and staff do not act to resolve the problems, score *No*.

5.2. Score *No* if staff solve children's social problems in a negative way, such as by removing a toy so that children cannot share, forcing sharing so a child's play is disrupted, or punishing a child who was too rough with a companion. If no problem is observed, score *Yes*.

5.3. "Few if any" means that throughout the observation children get along well and there are not many problems observed between children. When major problems do occur, teachers act quickly to resolve the problem so that there is no lasting undue distress. When scoring, be sure to account for when children get along well, and do not only consider the numbers of negative interactions observed.

7.2. The intent of this Indicator is to prevent problems between children, not simply to stop them when they do occur. To score this Indicator *Yes*, the observer should see signs indicating that the staff are sensitive to children's personalities, activities, and interactions.

7.3. Do not count "clean up" as an example of meeting this requirement. To score *Yes*, evidence must be observed, either in what is seen in the classroom or in activities in which children participate during the observation. To give credit, staff must have set up or suggested the project.

31. Peer interaction

1.1 Children are in staff-directed groups most of the time, and have little opportunity to choose their own companions or activities.

1.2 There is little or no staff guidance for positive interaction among children (Ex: staff intervene only if children are fighting or crying; many conflicts among children over toys; child with behavioral disability not watched carefully).

1.3 Interaction among children is usually negative (Ex: bullying, teasing, or fighting over toys or space are common).

3.1 Children have some time to select their own companions and activities during the observation (Ex: some free play is observed, indoors or outdoors).

3.2 Staff quickly stop hurtful peer interaction or none is observed (Ex: usually stop fighting, name-calling, or bullying, and only mild occurrences are missed).*

3.3 Staff generally model good social skills (Ex: are rarely bossy; are polite; respond when others talk to them; do not hurt others physically or emotionally; are not irritable).

5.1 Peer interaction is evident during at least half of the observation (Ex: plenty of time to self-select companions; children can choose who to sit with at lunch; some activities set up for children to be successful in cooperative play).

5.2 Staff generally help the children solve social problems in a satisfying way (Ex: help children take turns with a tricycle; help shy child find a chair to join in an art activity; redirect disruptive children to a more constructive activity).*

5.3 Most peer interaction is positive, with few if any conflicts.*

7.1 Staff point out children's positive social behavior toward one another (Ex: praise children who help others, work together to create a block building, or share crayons without fighting).

7.2 Staff help children avoid conflicts (Ex: have a system for ensuring fair turns, such as a waiting list; provide enough popular choices during free play; notice when a problem is brewing and provide closer supervision).*

7.3 Staff provide some opportunities for children to work together on a project (Ex: a group of children work to cover a large mural paper with many drawings; make soup with many ingredients; cooperate to set up obstacle course).*

Notes for Clarification

1.1, 1.4, 3.4, 5.4, 7.3. If no children's negative behavior is observed, and this is not due to rigid control by staff, score 1.1 *No*, and 3.4, 5.4, and 7.3 *Yes*. If no negative behavior is observed, but this is due to the fact that children are rigidly controlled by staff, score 1.4 *Yes*, and 3.4, 5.4, and 7.3 *No*.

3.3. "Most" means more than half of the expectations.

32. Discipline

1.1 Severe method of discipline is used (Ex: spanking; shouting; confining children for long periods; yanking; withholding food or physical activity).*

1.2 Discipline is so lax that there is little order or control.

1.3 Expectations for children are usually inappropriate for their age and developmental level (Ex: little talking allowed; children frequently wait long periods with nothing engaging to do; children required to use mature social skills such as sharing, cooperating; children often unreasonably restricted).

1.4 Staff often respond with anger to what they perceive as children's negative behavior.*

3.1. Staff do not use severe methods of discipline.

3.2 Staff usually maintain enough control to prevent children from hurting themselves, others, or being destructive to the classroom materials or environment.

3.3 Most expectations for children are appropriate (Ex: few periods when children must be quiet; children have lots of time to play actively; child not expected to share if it will cause difficulty with the activity that child is doing).*

3.4 Few if any negative or angry responses from staff to what they perceive as children's inappropriate behavior (Ex: belittling; calling names; yelling; reprimanding).*

5.1 Children appear to be aware of classroom rules, and generally follow them with a reasonable amount of teacher control.

5.2 Staff explain reasons for why they cannot permit specific behaviors (Ex: "Please get down, I'm afraid you will fall and get hurt." "Hitting hurts. We can't hit in our class.") *Observe once; score* Yes *if no problems*

5.3 Expectations for children are always appropriate, with no troublesome instances observed causing undue distress for children.

5.4 Staff are never observed responding with anger or negativity towards children's inappropriate behavior.*

7.1 Staff call attention to children's feelings and the relationship between children's action and other's responses (Ex: "You gave him the crayon. That made him happy." "Look at her face. She is upset now.")

7.2 Staff almost always use child-friendly procedures to minimize problems (Ex: transitions handled quickly with little waiting; group times allow active participation; crowding is minimized).

7.3 Staff actively involve children in solving their conflicts and problems without telling them what to do (Ex: help children talk out problems and think of satisfying solutions; sensitize children to feelings of others).*

Note for Clarification

1.4. The 10 minutes is not cumulative, so shorter waiting times during the observation should not be combined to see if they add up to 10. "Engaging" means that children are interested and involved in the activity. For example, when the staff lead singing while children line up and wait, but few children participate with interest, consider this "not engaging." Similarly, if children are told to get a book and read, but few actually look at a book with interest, consider this "not engaging."

PROGRAM STRUCTURE

33. Transitions and waiting times

1.1 Transitions are usually (75%) chaotic (Ex: much aimless wandering between daily events; children fighting; not involved in clean-up).

1.2 Staff usually not prepared for what comes next in the schedule.

1.3 Staff provide inadequate supervision to keep children productively on task during transitions (Ex: give children minimal guidance; little follow-up; staff roles not coordinated; staff occupied with other tasks).

1.4 Children required to wait for 10 minutes or more during any transition, with nothing engaging to do (Ex: waiting at table to eat; waiting in line; waiting for teacher to begin circle time).*

3.1 No negative staff-child interactions observed during the transitions.

3.2 Staff prepared for next activity at least half of the time (Ex: food for meals ready; materials needed for play activity at-hand).

3.3 Staff usually provide enough supervision as needed with few problems during transitions (Ex: give children guidance on clean-up; move about room to ensure group is completing task; children supervised while waiting or lining up).

5.1 Transitions are usually smooth (Ex: teachers warn that clean-up time is coming; children complete clean-up reasonably well; children line up and go to next event without much trouble).

5.2 Staff almost always prepared for next activity.

5.3 Staff supervise and follow up carefully, making sure that all children are productively engaged during transitions (Ex: staff coordinate their roles to ensure all tasks are completed as needed with little delay; more attention given to more difficult tasks).

7.1 Transitions are often gradual or individualized (Ex: children can go outside while others are still getting ready; children can begin eating as soon as they sit at table; teacher begins circle time while some children are still cleaning up).

7.2 No waiting time of 3 minutes or longer during any observed transition.

Notes for Clarification

*In scoring this Item, consider all free play times observed, including in the classroom or other areas used by the children, such as outdoors or the gym.

1.1, 3.1, 5.1. The time requirement is prorated proportionally for programs operating for less than 3 hours (see chart on p. 10).

5.1. The 1-hour time requirements must be met indoors when weather does not permit outdoor play.

3.4, 5.3. To give credit for 3.4, all children must be observed to be satisfied with activities in which they are engaged. No child should be left without an interesting choice. However, if there are adequate choices, but a child wants to do just one popular activity, and it was already being done by others so that the child would have to wait, then it should be observed that staff help the child to find a satisfying alternative. If there is nothing to interest the child, thus leaving the child unengaged for a long period, then score *No*. This is in contrast to 5.3, where many interesting choices are accessible, with the items from the Activities subscale and Books items usually (but not necessarily always) given credit for having the required amounts of materials. It should feel as if there is a wealth of choices for the children, from which there are many interesting possibilities for satisfying active play. Consider active play times as well as other indoor free play times.

5.2. If one or more areas that children use are often ignored or given very little teacher attention, score *No*. If much talk with children is not about their play, but instead involves directing children, managing their behavior, or quizzing them, score *No*. Less conversations are expected during active physical play times than during free play in centers, but some should be observed in order to give credit.

5.4. Watch to see if the system works well and allows children to play in an area or with another material while they wait. Children should feel at ease about being able to participate at some later time, even if not necessarily during the observation. Credit can be given if no obvious system is used but there are no problems and all children have satisfying choices.

Inadequate		Minimal		Good		Excellent
1	2	3	4	5	6	7

34. Free play*

1.1 Less than 25 minutes of free play is provided during the observation (Ex: most time is spent in groups, transitions, or routines).*

1.2 Little or no teacher interaction during free play.

1.3 Not enough time for children to complete the activities they choose (Ex: children given limited time to play before being required to change activity; popular center quickly filled so other children do not get to participate).

1.4 Very few interesting materials accessible during free play for children to be engaged.

3.1 Children have at least 25 minutes of indoor free play during the observation.*

3.2 Staff provide some supervision of free play (Ex: stop arguments or dangerous play; ensure proper use of materials; help child find something to do).

3.3 Children can usually complete activities to their satisfaction before being required to move to another activity (Ex: turns for new and popular activities are time-limited, and other interesting options exist; enough time allowed to complete activity before having to clean up for lunch).

3.4 There are generally enough interesting materials/activities/ space so that children can find something satisfying to do.*

5.1 Free play takes place for at least 1 hour during the observation, including some time inside and some outside, weather permitting.*

5.2 Staff frequently interact positively with children during free play (Ex: have conversations about things that interest them; talk about how play activity relates to other experiences).*

5.3 Ample and varied materials and equipment accessible for free play, so that children are able to find engaging activities with little if any competition.*

5.4 A clear system is used to permit satisfying participation in activities (Ex: timer used to limit turns to a reasonable time so that activity can be completed; waiting list used to ensure all interested children get a turn).*

7.1 Materials or activities accessible that relate to topics of interest/ current themes).

7.2 Staff use a wide variety of words to expand children's knowledge during free play activities.

7.3 Staff generally show awareness of whole group, even when working with one child or a small group (Ex: staff frequently scan room when working with one child; make sure area not visible is supervised by another staff member).

Notes for Clarification

*"Whole-group activities" are play and other learning activities where all children basically do the same thing at the same time. Such activities can be done with all children together in one big group, such as at circle time. They can also be done with children working at small tables, or even at separate desks all doing the same activity.

Score *NA* if no whole-group activities are ever used. The observation should be long enough to observe any group time that does occur during the active part of the day, when most children are present. If group times occur outside of the classroom, such as special art, music, or physical education classes for all children present, follow the group and include what is observed in scoring this item.

At higher levels of quality whole groups may be reduced in size; for example, by having half of the class stay indoors for whole-group activity while the other half goes outdoors to play. *Group activities do not include routines or transitions.*

5.2. If all children participate and there are no problems observed, and this is not due to strict, restrictive management of the children, score *Yes*. If the needs of all children are being met, and all are engaged with no extra support needed, score *Yes*.

Inadequate		Minimal		Good		Excellent
1	2	3	4	5	6	7

35. Whole-group activities for play and learning*

1.1 Content of learning activities required in group is often too difficult for most children, or not interesting to them.

1.2 Group activities are carried out in a way that creates problems for children (Ex: staff speak in monotone voice; children can't see what they are supposed to be learning about; not comfortable; have to listen to peers for too long).

1.3 Activities used require only passive, rather than active involvement (Ex: children mainly have to sit, listen, and look).

1.4 Staff are usually negative with children who have difficulty participating according to staff expectations.

3.1 Content of most group activities is somewhat interesting to most children in the group (Ex: not too hard or easy; most children behave well; few reminders needed by staff to get children's attention).

3.2 Group activities are set up with the basics to encourage child engagement (Ex: crowding does not cause problems; children can see book being read; no long periods when children must sit and just listen without active participation).

3.3 Some active involvement included for children in group activities (Ex: singing; exercise; group response to questions).

3.4 Staff are rarely negative with children who have trouble participating, and do not cause undue distress when reminding them to pay attention.

5.1 Staff are responsive and flexible in ways that maximize child engagement (Ex: stop story and move to a more active experience when children have trouble sitting still; staff speak with animation; avoid having children listen to peers for long periods).

5.2 Staff provide support for children who have trouble participating (Ex: allow child to hold toy to keep hands busy while participating; child can sit on adult's lap or chair).*

5.3 Staff use group times to introduce children to meaningful ideas in which children are interested (Ex: review theme of the week; explain how to use new material; tell children what will happen on field trip).

7.1 All children in the group are actively engaged in group activities.

7.2 Group activities are usually carried out in smaller groups, rather than in one large group (Ex: younger children or those who have trouble attending are placed in smaller groups).

7.3 Children in large group are allowed to leave whole group in order to work in another area that is more satisfying to them.

Notes

SCORESHEET

Early Childhood Environment Rating Scale–Third Edition
Thelma Harms, Ellen V. Jacobs, and Donna R. White

Observer: _____

Observer Code: ___ ___ ___

Date of Observation: ___ ___ / ___ ___ / ___ ___
                        m m   d d   y y

Center/School: _____

Center Code: ___ ___ ___

Number of children with identified disabilities: ___ ___

Room: _____

Room Code: ___ ___

Check type(s) of disability:
☐ physical/sensory   ☐ cognitive/language
☐ social/emotional   ☐ other: _____

Teacher(s): _____

Teacher Code: ___ ___ ___

Birthdates of children enrolled:
youngest ___ ___ / ___ ___ / ___ ___
                    m m   d d   y y
oldest   ___ ___ / ___ ___ / ___ ___
                  m m   d d   y y

Time				
# of staff present				
# of children present				

Highest number center allows in class at one time: ___ ___

Number enrolled: ___ ___

Highest number of children present during observation: ___ ___

Number of childen under 3 years of age in this class: ___ ___

Do any children in the group have food allergies? _____

Do any families have food preferences? _____

Time observation began: ___ ___ : ___ ___ ☐ AM ☐ PM

Time observation ended: ___ ___ : ___ ___ ☐ AM ☐ PM

What space(s) are used for gross motor activities for this class?

_____

Which gross motor spaces are used most often (indoors or outdoors)?

_____

SPACE AND FURNISHINGS

1. Indoor space

1 2 3 4 5 6 7

	Y N		Y N		Y N		Y N
1.1	☐ ☐	3.1	☐ ☐	5.1	☐ ☐	7.1	☐ ☐
1.2	☐ ☐	3.2	☐ ☐	5.2	☐ ☐	7.2	☐ ☐
1.3	☐ ☐	3.3	☐ ☐	5.3	☐ ☐	7.3	☐ ☐
1.4	☐ ☐	3.4	☐ ☐				
		3.5	☐ ☐				

2. Furnishings for care, play, and learning [1 2 3 4 5 6 7]

Y N	Y N	Y N	Y N
1.1 ☐ ☐	3.1 ☐ ☐	5.1 ☐ ☐	7.1 ☐ ☐
1.2 ☐ ☐	3.2 ☐ ☐	5.2 ☐ ☐	7.2 ☐ ☐
1.3 ☐ ☐	3.3 ☐ ☐	5.3 ☐ ☐	7.3 ☐ ☐
	3.4 ☐ ☐	5.4 ☐ ☐	

5.2. Child-sized? _____ (# child-sized) ÷ _____ (# children) = _____ (% child-sized)

3. Room arrangement for play and learning [1 2 3 4 5 6 7]

List defined interest centers:

Y N NA	Y N NA	Y N NA	Y N
1.1 ☐ ☐ ☐	3.1 ☐ ☐ ☐	5.1 ☐ ☐ ☐	7.1 ☐ ☐
1.2 ☐ ☐ ☐	3.2 ☐ ☐ ☐	5.2 ☐ ☐ ☐	7.2 ☐ ☐
1.3 ☐ ☐ ☐	3.3 ☐ ☐ ☐	5.3 ☐ ☐ ☐	7.3 ☐ ☐
1.4 ☐ ☐ ☐	3.4 ☐ ☐ ☐	5.4 ☐ ☐ ☐	

4. Space for privacy [1 2 3 4 5 6 7]

Y N	Y N	Y N	Y N
1.1 ☐ ☐	3.1 ☐ ☐	5.1 ☐ ☐	7.1 ☐ ☐
1.2 ☐ ☐	3.2 ☐ ☐	5.2 ☐ ☐	7.2 ☐ ☐
1.3 ☐ ☐		5.3 ☐ ☐	

5. Child-related display [1 2 3 4 5 6 7]

Y N	Y N	Y N	Y N
1.1 ☐ ☐	3.1 ☐ ☐	5.1 ☐ ☐	7.1 ☐ ☐
1.2 ☐ ☐	3.2 ☐ ☐	5.2 ☐ ☐	7.2 ☐ ☐
1.3 ☐ ☐	3.3 ☐ ☐	5.3 ☐ ☐	7.3 ☐ ☐
		5.4 ☐ ☐	7.4 ☐ ☐

6. Space for gross motor play

$$\boxed{1 \quad 2 \quad 3 \quad 4 \quad 5 \quad 6 \quad 7}$$

	Y	N		Y	N		Y	N		Y	N
1.1	☐	☐	3.1	☐	☐	5.1	☐	☐	7.1	☐	☐
1.2	☐	☐	3.2	☐	☐	5.2	☐	☐	7.2	☐	☐
1.3	☐	☐				5.3	☐	☐	7.3	☐	☐
						5.4	☐	☐			

7. Gross motor equipment

$$\boxed{1 \quad 2 \quad 3 \quad 4 \quad 5 \quad 6 \quad 7}$$

	Y	N		Y	N		Y	N	NA		Y	N
1.1	☐	☐	3.1	☐	☐	5.1	☐	☐		7.1	☐	☐
1.2	☐	☐	3.2	☐	☐	5.2	☐	☐		7.2	☐	☐
1.3	☐	☐	3.3	☐	☐	5.3	☐	☐		7.3	☐	☐
						5.4	☐	☐	☐			

A. Subscale (Items 1–7) Score __ __   B. Number of Items scored __ __   **SPACE AND FURNISHINGS** Average Score (A ÷ B) __.__ __

PERSONAL CARE ROUTINES

8. Meals/snacks

$$\boxed{1 \quad 2 \quad 3 \quad 4 \quad 5 \quad 6 \quad 7}$$

	Y	N		Y	N		Y	N		Y	N
1.1	☐	☐	3.1	☐	☐	5.1	☐	☐	7.1	☐	☐
1.2	☐	☐	3.2	☐	☐	5.2	☐	☐	7.2	☐	☐
1.3	☐	☐	3.3	☐	☐	5.3	☐	☐	7.3	☐	☐
						5.4	☐	☐			
						5.5	☐	☐			

9. Toileting/diapering

$$\boxed{1 \quad 2 \quad 3 \quad 4 \quad 5 \quad 6 \quad 7}$$

	Y	N		Y	N		Y	N		Y	N
1.1	☐	☐	3.1	☐	☐	5.1	☐	☐	7.1	☐	☐
1.2	☐	☐	3.2	☐	☐	5.2	☐	☐	7.2	☐	☐
1.3	☐	☐	3.3	☐	☐	5.3	☐	☐	7.3	☐	☐
			3.4	☐	☐						

10. Health practices | 1 2 3 4 5 6 7 |

Handwashing observed:

Upon arrival in class or re-entry from outdoors:
After sand or play with messy dry materials:
Before/after water play or use of shared moist materials:
After dealing w/ bodily fluids or skin contact with open sores:
After touching pets or contaminated objects:

Y N NA	Y N NA	Y N	Y N
1.1 □ □ □	3.1 □ □ □	5.1 □ □	7.1 □ □
1.2 □ □ □	3.2 □ □ □	5.2 □ □	7.2 □ □
1.3 □ □ □	3.3 □ □ □	5.3 □ □	7.3 □ □

11. Safety practices | 1 2 3 4 5 6 7 |

1.1, 3.1. Safety hazards

	Major	Minor
Indoors		
Outdoors		

Y N NA	Y N NA	Y N	Y N
1.1 □ □ □	3.1 □ □ □	5.1 □ □	7.1 □ □
1.2 □ □ □	3.2 □ □ □	5.2 □ □	7.2 □ □
1.3 □ □ □	3.3 □ □ □	5.3 □ □	7.3 □ □
1.4 □ □ □	3.4 □ □ □		

A. Subscale (Items 8–11) Score ___ . ___ ___   B. Number of Items scored ___   **PERSONAL CARE ROUTINES Average Score (A ÷ B)** ___ . ___ ___

LANGUAGE AND LITERACY

12. Helping children expand vocabulary | 1 2 3 4 5 6 7 |

5.2. Explain meaning of word (2 examples):

7.3. Expansion (2 examples):

Y N	Y N NA	Y N	Y N
1.1 □ □	3.1 □ □	5.1 □ □	7.1 □ □
1.2 □ □	3.2 □ □	5.2 □ □	7.2 □ □
1.3 □ □	3.3 □ □	5.3 □ □	7.3 □ □
		5.4 □ □	

13. Encouraging children to use language

| | 1 2 3 4 5 6 7 |

	Y N		Y N		Y N		Y N
1.1	☐ ☐	3.1	☐ ☐	5.1	☐ ☐	7.1	☐ ☐
1.2	☐ ☐	3.2	☐ ☐	5.2	☐ ☐	7.2	☐ ☐
1.3	☐ ☐	3.3	☐ ☐	5.3	☐ ☐	7.3	☐ ☐
1.4	☐ ☐	3.4	☐ ☐	5.4	☐ ☐		
1.5	☐ ☐	3.5	☐ ☐				

5.4. Encourage social talk with other children (not with adults) (2 examples):

7.1. Staff questions to explain or expand (2 examples):

7.3. Staff/child conversations beyond class activities (1 example):

14. Staff use of books with children

| | 1 2 3 4 5 6 7 |

	Y N		Y N		Y N		Y N
1.1	☐ ☐	3.1	☐ ☐	5.1	☐ ☐	7.1	☐ ☐
1.2	☐ ☐	3.2	☐ ☐	5.2	☐ ☐	7.2	☐ ☐
1.3	☐ ☐	3.3	☐ ☐	5.3	☐ ☐	7.3	☐ ☐
1.4	☐ ☐	3.4	☐ ☐	5.4	☐ ☐	7.4	☐ ☐

7.1. Use of books that relate to current class activities (1 example):

7.2. Staff and children discuss book content (1 example):

7.3. Books used informally (2 examples):

7.4. Use books to help answer questions (1 example):

15. Encouraging children's use of books

| | 1 2 3 4 5 6 7 |

	Y N		Y N		Y N		Y N
1.1	☐ ☐	3.1	☐ ☐	5.1	☐ ☐	7.1	☐ ☐
1.2	☐ ☐	3.2	☐ ☐	5.2	☐ ☐	7.2	☐ ☐
1.3	☐ ☐	3.3	☐ ☐	5.3	☐ ☐	7.3	☐ ☐
1.4	☐ ☐	3.4	☐ ☐	5.4	☐ ☐		

16. Becoming familiar with print

| 1 2 3 4 5 6 7 |

	Y N		Y N		Y N		Y N
1.1	☐ ☐	3.1	☐ ☐	5.1	☐ ☐	7.1	☐ ☐
1.2	☐ ☐	3.2	☐ ☐	5.2	☐ ☐	7.2	☐ ☐
1.3	☐ ☐	3.3	☐ ☐	5.3	☐ ☐	7.3	☐ ☐
1.4	☐ ☐					7.4	☐ ☐

1.4. Observe 2 examples.

3.2. Observe 1 example.

5.3. Observe 1 example.

7.2. Observe 2 examples.

7.4. Observe 1 example.

A. Subscale (Items 12–16) Score __ __   B. Number of Items scored __ __   **LANGUAGE AND LITERACY Average Score (A ÷ B)** __.__ __

LEARNING ACTIVITIES

17. Fine motor

| 1 2 3 4 5 6 7 |

	Y N		Y N		Y N		Y N
1.1	☐ ☐	3.1	☐ ☐	5.1	☐ ☐	7.1	☐ ☐
1.2	☐ ☐	3.2	☐ ☐	5.2	☐ ☐	7.2	☐ ☐
1.3	☐ ☐	3.3	☐ ☐	5.3	☐ ☐	7.3	☐ ☐
		3.4	☐ ☐				

Types of fine motor material
(total of 10 required for 3.1; all categories must be represented for 5.1):

• Interlocking building materials:

• Art:

• Manipulatives:

• Puzzles:

7.1. Staff show extended interest in children's use of fine motor materials
(Observe for 2 children):

18. Art

| 1 2 3 4 5 6 7 |

	Y N		Y N		Y N		Y N
1.1	☐ ☐	3.1	☐ ☐	5.1	☐ ☐	7.1	☐ ☐
1.2	☐ ☐	3.2	☐ ☐	5.2	☐ ☐	7.2	☐ ☐
1.3	☐ ☐	3.3	☐ ☐	5.3	☐ ☐	7.3	☐ ☐

3.3. Positive staff involvement with art (1 example):

5.1. Types of art materials (list example[s] for each):

• Drawing:

• Paints: • 3-D:

• Collage: • Tools:

5.3. Staff-child conversations about art (2 examples):

7.3. Staff write captions (1 example):

19. Music and movement

1	2	3	4	5	6	7

	Y N		Y N NA		Y N		Y N NA
1.1	☐ ☐	3.1	☐ ☐	5.1	☐ ☐	7.1	☐ ☐ ☐
1.2	☐ ☐	3.2	☐ ☐	5.2	☐ ☐	7.2	☐ ☐
		3.3	☐ ☐	5.3	☐ ☐	7.3	☐ ☐ ☐
		3.4	☐ ☐ ☐	5.4	☐ ☐		

Types of music materials (3 needed for 3.1; 10 needed for 5.1):

• instruments:

• music to listen to (played by staff or child):

7.2. Point out rhyming words in songs, etc. (1 example):

7.3. Experiment with rhyming in songs (1 example):

20. Blocks

1	2	3	4	5	6	7

	Y N		Y N		Y N		Y N
1.1	☐ ☐	3.1	☐ ☐	5.1	☐ ☐	7.1	☐ ☐
1.2	☐ ☐	3.2	☐ ☐	5.2	☐ ☐	7.2	☐ ☐
		3.3	☐ ☐	5.3	☐ ☐	7.3	☐ ☐
		3.4	☐ ☐	5.4	☐ ☐		
				5.5	☐ ☐		

Types of blocks (√ = observed):

__ unit

__ large hollow

7.2. Link written language to block play (1 example, evidence in display can count):

7.3. Staff points out math concepts related to blocks (1 example):

21. Dramatic play

1	2	3	4	5	6	7

	Y N		Y N		Y N		Y N
1.1	☐ ☐	3.1	☐ ☐	5.1	☐ ☐	7.1	☐ ☐
1.2	☐ ☐	3.2	☐ ☐	5.2	☐ ☐	7.2	☐ ☐
1.3	☐ ☐	3.3	☐ ☐	5.3	☐ ☐		

5.1. Themes represented in props (2 examples):

5.3. Observe two conversations:

7.1. Diversity (4 examples):

7.2. Number talk in dramatic play (1 example):

24. Math in daily events

1 2 3 4 5 6 7

Y N	Y N NA	Y N	Y N NA
1.1 ☐ ☐	3.1 ☐ ☐ ☐	5.1 ☐ ☐	7.1 ☐ ☐
1.2 ☐ ☐	3.2 ☐ ☐ ☐	5.2 ☐ ☐	7.2 ☐ ☐
1.3 ☐ ☐	3.3 ☐ ☐ ☐		7.3 ☐ ☐

3.1/5.1. Count/use math words during transitions and routines (1 example required for 3.1; 2 example required for 5.1):

3.2/5.2. Math talk during play with non-math materials (1 example required for 3.2; 2 required for 5.2):

3.3. Math talk about daily events (1 example):

7.1. Connect print number/shape with use in environment (1 example):

7.2. Children explain math reasoning (1 example):

7.3. More complex tasks for older children (1 example):

23. Math materials and activities

1 2 3 4 5 6 7

Y N	Y N	Y N	Y N
1.1 ☐ ☐	3.1 ☐ ☐	5.1 ☐ ☐	7.1 ☐ ☐
1.2 ☐ ☐	3.2 ☐ ☐	5.2 ☐ ☐	7.2 ☐ ☐
1.3 ☐ ☐	3.3 ☐ ☐	5.3 ☐ ☐	7.3 ☐ ☐
		5.4 ☐ ☐	

3.2. Staff give info and ask questions:

5.2. Join in math materials play, ask questions, respond, show enthusiasm (3 examples):

7.2. Questioning that stimulates reasoning with materials (1 example):

7.3. Math activities with teacher input (1 example):

3.1/5.1. Types of math/number materials (3.1 requires 2 from each category; 5.1 requires 10 total, with 3 from each category):
- Counting/comparing quantities:
- Measuring/comparing sizes, parts of whole:
- Familiarity with shapes:

22. Nature/science

1 2 3 4 5 6 7

Y N	Y N	Y N	Y N
1.1 ☐ ☐	3.1 ☐ ☐	5.1 ☐ ☐	7.1 ☐ ☐
1.2 ☐ ☐	3.2 ☐ ☐	5.2 ☐ ☐	7.2 ☐ ☐
1.3 ☐ ☐	3.3 ☐ ☐	5.3 ☐ ☐	

3.1/5.1. Types of nature/science materials (5 from 2 types required for 3.1; 15 from 5 types required for 5.1):

Living things: Tools:

Natural objects: Sand/water:

Factual books, picture games (5 books required):

3.2. Talk about nature/science in any way (1 example):

5.2. Talk about nature/science as children use materials (1 example):

5.3. Model care/respect for environment (1 example):

7.2. Help care for and talk about pet/plant (1 example):

25. Understanding written numbers

| 1 | 2 | 3 | 4 | 5 | 6 | 7 |

	Y	N		Y	N		Y	N		Y	N
1.1	☐	☐	3.1	☐	☐	5.1	☐	☐	7.1	☐	☐
1.2	☐	☐	3.2	☐	☐	5.2	☐	☐	7.2	☐	☐
1.3	☐	☐	3.3	☐	☐	5.3	☐	☐	7.3	☐	☐
			3.4	☐	☐				7.4	☐	☐

3.3. Point out numbers on play materials (1 example):

3.4. Relate print number to number of objects or pictures (1 example):

5.1, 7.1. Play materials accessible showing print numbers and things to count (5.1 requires 3 examples; 7.1 requires 5 examples):

5.3, 7.3. Show children how to use materials with print numbers and talk about meaning (5.3 requires 1 example; 7.3 requires 2 examples):

7.4. Relate print number to number of fingers (1 example):

---

26. Promoting acceptance of diversity

| 1 | 2 | 3 | 4 | 5 | 6 | 7 |

	Y	N		Y	N		Y	N		Y	N
1.1	☐	☐	3.1	☐	☐	5.1	☐	☐	7.1	☐	☐
1.2	☐	☐	3.2	☐	☐	5.2	☐	☐	7.2	☐	☐
1.3	☐	☐	3.3	☐	☐	5.3	☐	☐			

3.1, 5.2. Examples of diversity in materials:

___ Books ___ Pictures ____ Dolls and Other play materials

Total (3 required for 3.1; 10 required for 5.2):

5.1. Two types of dramatic play props showing diversity:

5.3. Types of diversity represented (Check if found):

Race___ Culture___ Age___ Ability___ Gender___

7.1. Diversity in learning activities (1 example):

7.2. Positive conversations about benefits of similarities and differences (1 example):

---

27. Appropriate use of technology

| 1 | 2 | 3 | 4 | 5 | 6 | 7 | NA |

	Y	N		Y	N	NA		Y	N	NA		Y	N
1.1	☐	☐	3.1	☐	☐		5.1	☐	☐		7.1	☐	☐
1.2	☐	☐	3.2	☐	☐	☐	5.2	☐	☐	☐	7.2	☐	☐
1.3	☐	☐	3.3	☐	☐		5.3	☐	☐	☐			
							5.4	☐	☐				

5.4. Staff actively involved? (1 example)

A. Subscale (Items 17–27) Score __ __   B. Number of Items scored __ __   **LEARNING ACTIVITIES Average Score (A ÷ B)** __.__ __

INTERACTION

28. Supervision of gross motor
1 2 3 4 5 6 7

Y N	Y N	Y N	Y N
1.1	3.1	5.1	7.1
1.2	3.2	5.2	7.2
1.3	3.3	5.3	

29. Individualized teaching and learning
1 2 3 4 5 6 7

Y N	Y N	Y N	Y N
1.1	3.1	5.1	7.1
1.2	3.2	5.2	7.2
1.3	3.3	5.3	
1.4	3.4		

30. Staff-child interaction
1 2 3 4 5 6 7

Y N	Y N	Y N	Y N
1.1	3.1	5.1	7.1
1.2	3.2	5.2	7.2
1.3	3.3	5.3	7.3
1.4			

31. Peer interaction
1 2 3 4 5 6 7

Y N	Y N	Y N	Y N
1.1	3.1	5.1	7.1
1.2	3.2	5.2	7.2
1.3	3.3	5.3	7.3

32. Discipline

1 2 3 4 5 6 7

	Y N		Y N		Y N		Y N
1.1	☐ ☐	3.1	☐ ☐	5.1	☐ ☐	7.1	☐ ☐
1.2	☐ ☐	3.2	☐ ☐	5.2	☐ ☐	7.2	☐ ☐
1.3	☐ ☐	3.3	☐ ☐	5.3	☐ ☐	7.3	☐ ☐
1.4	☐ ☐	3.4	☐ ☐	5.4	☐ ☐		

A. Subscale (Items 28–32) Score __ __   B. Number of Items scored __ __   **INTERACTION Average Score (A ÷ B)** __.__ __

PROGRAM STRUCTURE

33. Transitions and waiting times

1 2 3 4 5 6 7

	Y N		Y N		Y N		Y N
1.1	☐ ☐	3.1	☐ ☐	5.1	☐ ☐	7.1	☐ ☐
1.2	☐ ☐	3.2	☐ ☐	5.2	☐ ☐	7.2	☐ ☐
1.3	☐ ☐	3.3	☐ ☐	5.3	☐ ☐		
1.4	☐ ☐						

34. Free play

1 2 3 4 5 6 7

	Y N		Y N		Y N		Y N
1.1	☐ ☐	3.1	☐ ☐	5.1	☐ ☐	7.1	☐ ☐
1.2	☐ ☐	3.2	☐ ☐	5.2	☐ ☐	7.2	☐ ☐
1.3	☐ ☐	3.3	☐ ☐	5.3	☐ ☐	7.3	☐ ☐
1.4	☐ ☐	3.4	☐ ☐	5.4	☐ ☐		

35. Whole-group activities for play and learning

1 2 3 4 5 6 7 NA

	Y N		Y N		Y N		Y N
1.1	☐ ☐	3.1	☐ ☐	5.1	☐ ☐	7.1	☐ ☐
1.2	☐ ☐	3.2	☐ ☐	5.2	☐ ☐	7.2	☐ ☐
1.3	☐ ☐	3.3	☐ ☐	5.3	☐ ☐	7.3	☐ ☐
1.4	☐ ☐	3.4	☐ ☐				

A. Subscale (Items 33–35) Score __ __   B. Number of Items scored __ __   **PROGRAM STRUCTURE Average Score (A ÷ B)** __.__ __

TOTAL AND AVERAGE SCORES

	Score	# of Items Scored	Average Score
Space and Furnishings			
Personal Care Routines			
Language and Literacy			
Learning Activities			
Interaction			
Program Structure			
TOTAL			

Observed Schedule

ECERS-3 Profile

Center/School: _____

Teacher(s)/Classroom: _____

Observer(s): _____

Observation 1: ___ ___ / ___ ___ / ___ ___
            m m   d d   y y

Observation 2: ___ ___ / ___ ___ / ___ ___
            m m   d d   y y

Observer(s): _____

I. Space and Furnishings (1–7)

1. Indoor space
2. Furnishings for care, play, and learning
3. Room arrangement for play and learning
4. Space for privacy
5. Child-related display
6. Space for gross motor play
7. Gross motor equipment

Obs. 1 □   Obs. 2 □   Average Subscale Score □

II. Personal Care Routines (8–11)

8. Meals/snacks
9. Toileting/diapering
10. Health practices
11. Safety practices

□ □

III. Language and Literacy (12–16)

12. Helping children expand vocabulary
13. Encouraging children to use language
14. Staff use of books with children
15. Encouraging children's use of books
16. Becoming familiar with print

□ □

IV. Learning Activities (17–27)

17. Fine motor
18. Art
19. Music and movement
20. Blocks
21. Dramatic play
22. Nature/science
23. Math materials and activities
24. Math in daily events
25. Understanding written numbers
26. Promoting acceptance of diversity
27. Appropriate use of technology

□ □

V. Interaction (28–32)

28. Supervision of gross motor
29. Individualized teaching and learning
30. Staff-child interaction
31. Peer interaction
32. Discipline

□ □

VI. Program Structure (33–35)

33. Transitions and waiting times
34. Free play
35. Whole-group activities for play and learning

□ □

Average Subscale Scores

SPACE AND FURNISHINGS
PERSONAL CARE ROUTINES
LANGUAGE AND LITERACY
LEARNING ACTIVITIES
INTERACTION
PROGRAM STRUCTURE

1 2 3 4 5 6 7

Additional Information

Additional Information

Additional Information